ZEN KEYS

ZEN KEYS

THICH NHAT HANH

With an Introduction by
PHILIP KAPLEAU

DOUBLEDAY
New York   London
Toronto   Sydney   Auckland

AN IMAGE BOOK
PUBLISHED BY DOUBLEDAY
a division of Bantam Doubleday Dell Publishing Group, Inc.
1540 Broadway, New York, New York 10036

IMAGE, DOUBLEDAY, and the portrayal of a deer drinking from a stream
are trademarks of Doubleday, a division of Bantam Doubleday Dell
Publishing Group, Inc.

Zen Keys was originally published in French as Clefs pour le Zen by
Éditions Seghers, © Éditions Seghers, Paris, 1973.

First published in the English language by Anchor Books, Doubleday,
1974. This Image edition published January 1995.

Library of Congress Cataloging-in-Publication Data
Nhât Hạnh, Thích.
[Clefs pour le zen. English]
Zen Keys / Thich Nhat Hanh ; introduction by Philip Kapleau.
p. cm.
Originally published: Garden City, N.Y. : Anchor Press, 1974.
.1. Zen Buddhism—Essence, genius, nature. I. Title.
BQ9265.9.N4513   1994
294.3′927—dc20   94–1620
                                                                 CIP

ISBN 0-385-47561-6
Translation copyright © 1974 by Doubleday & Company, Inc.
Introduction copyright © 1974, 1995 by Philip Kapleau
Revisions copyright © 1995 by Thich Nhat Hanh

Book design by Claire Naylon Vaccaro

CONTENTS

INTRODUCTION

The publication in English of Thich[1] Nhat Hanh's *Zen Keys* has particular significance for Americans. For not only is his work the first precise statement of Vietnamese Buddhism to come to us—we who have such a deep and tragic karmic connection with Vietnam—but also Thich Nhat Hanh is not an average Buddhist. He is a Zen monk, trained and developed in a Zen monastery, a man who has realized the wisdom and compassion which are the fruits of Buddhist practice. Over the past thirty-five years Thich Nhat Hanh, one of the leading spokesmen of the Vietnamese Buddhist peace movement, has taken himself into the market place, into the twentieth-century hell of war-ravaged Vietnam, and brought an "engaged" Buddhism into the mainstream of life of the Vietnamese masses and to many others around the world. In the face of threats of persecution, imprisonment, and even death, he has repeatedly spoken out, urging others to avoid

---

[1] "Thich" is not, as many suppose, the Vietnamese equivalent of "Venerable," an appellation of Buddhist monks that roughly corresponds to "Reverend," but is the shortened form of "Thich-Ca," the Vietnamese for Shakya, which is the abbreviation of Shakyamuni, the name by which the Buddha is known in Asia. It is a family name that monks and nuns assume upon ordination, replacing their own.

hatred and acrimony and insisting that the real enemy is not man but the grenades of greed, anger, and delusion in the human heart. Those Americans who believe Buddhism is a world-denying cult of inner illumination and its practice of meditation a navel-gazing escape from the sufferings of life do not know Thich Nhat Hanh or the Buddhism about which he writes. It is important that American readers, before delving deeply into this book, be aware of these aspects of its author's life.

It is well to note that while *Zen Keys* often presents weighty aspects of Buddhist philosophy, Nhat Hanh begins his book with the concrete, practical aspects of life in a Zen monastery, where the emphasis is not on the learning of philosophic concepts but on simple labor and a life of aware- ness. For in Zen, intellectual learning is nothing but the study- ing of the menu, while actual practice is the eating of the meal. As Nhat Hanh says, the truth of existence is revealed through a deepening awareness that comes from living a life of single-mindedness, of being "awake" in whatever one is doing. There is no better laboratory for doing this "aware work" than everyday life, especially one's daily work.

Yet we live in a society where the object for so many is to do as little work as possible, where the workplace, whether office or home, is looked upon as a place of drudgery and boredom, where work rather than being a creative and fulfill- ing aspect of one's life is seen as oppressive and unsatisfying. How different is this from Zen! In Zen everything one does becomes a vehicle for self-realization; every act, every movement is done wholeheartedly, with nothing left over. In Zen parlance, everything we do this way is an "expression of Buddha," and the greater the single-mindedness and unself-consciousness of the doing, the closer we are to this realization. For what else is there but the pure act—the lifting of the hammer, the washing of the dish, the movement of the hands on the typewriter, the pulling of the weed? Everything else— thoughts of the past, fantasies about the future, judgments and evaluations concerning the work itself—what are these but shadows and ghosts flickering about in our minds, preventing us from entering fully into life itself? To enter into the awareness of Zen, to "wake up," means to cleanse the mind of the habitual disease of uncontrolled thought and to bring it back to its original state of purity and clarity. In Zen it is said that more power is generated by the ability to practice in the midst of the world than by just sitting alone and shunning all activity. Thus, one's daily work becomes one's meditation room; the task at hand one's practice. This is called "working for oneself."

In Zen all labor is viewed with the eye of equality, for it is nothing but the workings of a dualistically ensnared mind that discriminates between agreeable and disagreeable jobs, between creative and uncreative work. It is to root out this weighing and judging that Zen novices are set to work pulling weeds by hand, licking envelopes, or doing other seemingly unimportant "non-creative" work at the start of their training, and why the abbot himself often cleans the toilets. For true creativity is possible only when the mind is empty and totally absorbed in the task at hand. Only at the point where one is freed of the weight of self-consciousness in the complete identification with work is there transcendence and the joy of fulfillment. In this type of creativity our intuitive wisdom and joy are naturally brought into play.

All this does not mean, of course, that attempts at bettering working conditions and making work more meaningful, such as we are witnessing today as a reaction against robotlike mechanization of the workplace, are worthless. But for a worker constantly to resent his work or his superiors, for him to become sloppy and slothful in his working habits, for him to become embittered toward life—these attitudes do most harm to the worker himself and serve little to change his working conditions. When it's time to work one works, nothing held back; when it's time to make changes one makes changes; when it's time to revolt one even revolts. In Zen everything is in the doing, not in the contemplating.

There is one more area in which the untrained, ego-dominated mind plays thief to man, and this is in terms of energy. The fatigue that grips many of us at the end of the workday is not a natural tiredness, but the product of a day filled with wasted thought and feelings of anxiety and worry, not to speak of anger and resentments openly expressed or inwardly held. These negative mental states probably do more to sap energy than anything else. In contrast, the trained Zen person moves through his daily round aware and alert. The task in hand receives its due share of his energy, but none is wasted in anxiety, fantasy, or smoldering resentment. Even at the end of a full day's work his store of energy is not exhausted.

Throughout *Zen Keys*, Thich Nhat Hanh stresses that mindfulness—and this is more than mere attentiveness—is everything. It is precisely the lack of mindfulness that is responsible for so much of the violence and suffering in the world today. For it is the mind that feels itself separated from life and nature, dominated by an omnipresent Ego-I that lashes out to destroy and kill, to satisfy its desire for more and more at whatever cost. It is the unaware mind that breeds insensitivity to people and things, for it doesn't see and appreciate the value of things as they are, only seeing them as objects to be used in satiating one's own desires. The aware person sees the indivisibility of existence, the deep complexity and interrelationship of all life, and this creates in him a deep respect for the absolute value of things. It is out of this respect for the worth of every single object, animate as well as inanimate, that comes the desire to see things used properly, and not to be heedless or wasteful or destructive. Truly to practice Zen therefore means never to leave lights burning when they are not needed, never to allow water to run unnecessarily in the faucet, never to leave a scrap of food uneaten. For not only are these unmindful acts, but they indicate an indifference to the value of the object wasted or destroyed and to the efforts of those who made it possible for us: in the case of food, the farmer, the trucker, the storekeeper, the cook, the server. This indifference is the product of a mind that sees itself as separated from a world of seemingly random change and purpose-less chaos.

From a Buddhist point of view the doctrines of imperma-nence and not-self, with which Nhat Hanh deals, hold the key to resolving the anxiety of this isolated point of view. Anyone alive to the realities of life cannot but acknowledge, for exam-ple, that impermanence is not a creation of mystical philoso-phers but simply a concretization of what "is." In the last hun-dred years this process of constant and explosive change on the social and institutional level has accelerated to a degree unknown to people of earlier ages. Almost daily the newspa-pers report new and dizzying crises in the world: famines and natural disasters; wars and revolutions; crises in the environ-ment, in energy and in the political arena; crises in the world of finance and economics; crises in the increasing number of divorces and nervous breakdowns, crises in personal health, in the incidence of heart attacks, cancer, and other fatal diseases, not to mention the number of senseless deaths caused by the traffic in and extensive consumption of illegal drugs. Most people looking out on this ever-changing, seemingly chaotic world see anything but natural karmic laws at work, nor do they perceive the unity and harmony underlying this constant and inevitable change. If anything, they are filled with anxi-ety, with a feeling of powerlessness, and with a sense that life has no meaning. And because they have no concrete insight into the true character of the world or intuitive understanding of it, what else can they do but surrender to a life of material comfort and sensual pleasure? And yet right in the midst of this seemingly meaningless swirling chaos of change stand Zen Buddhists. Their equanimity is proof that they know there is more to life than what the senses tell them—that in the midst of change there is something that never changes, in the midst of impermanence there is something always permanent, in the midst of imperfection there is perfection, in chaos there is peace, in noise there is quiet, and, finally, in death there is life. So without holding on or pushing away, without accepting or rejecting, they just move along with their daily work, doing what needs to be done, helping wherever they can, or, as the sutras say, "In all things they are neither overjoyed nor cast down."

Like the law of impermanence, the doctrine of not-self is not the product of philosophical speculation but the expression of the deepest religious experience. It affirms that contrary to what we *think*, we are not merely a body or a mind. If not either or both, what are we? The Buddha's answer, stemming from his experience of Great Enlightenment, is ego shattering:

"In truth I say to you that within this fathom-high body, with its thoughts and perceptions, lies the world and the rising of the world and the ceasing of the world and the Way that leads to the extinction of rising and ceasing."

What could be grander or more reassuring? Here is confirmation from the highest source that we are more than this puny body-mind, more than a speck thrown into the vast universe by a capricious fate—that we are no less than the sun and the moon and the stars and the great earth. Why if we already possess the world in fee simple, do we try to enlarge ourselves through possessions and power? Why are we "alone and afraid in a world I never made," at times self-pitying and mean, at other times arrogant and aggressive? It is because our image of ourselves and our relation to the world is a false one. We are deceived by our limited five senses and discriminating intellect (the sixth sense in Buddhism) which convey to us a picture of a dualistic world of self-and-other, of things separated and isolated, of pain and struggle, birth and extinction, killing and being killed. This picture is untrue because it barely scratches the surface. It is like looking at the one eighth of an iceberg above the water and being unaware of the seven eighths underneath. For if we could see beyond the ever-changing forms into the underlying reality, we would realize that in essence there is nothing but harmony and unity and stability, and that this perfection is no different from the phenomenal world of incessant change and transformation. But our vision is limited and our intuitions weak.

Nor is this the whole of it. Sitting astride the senses is a shadowy, phantomlike figure with insatiable desires and a lust for dominance. His name? Ego, Ego the Magician, and the deadly tricks he carries up his sleeve are delusive thinking, greed, and anger. Where he came from no one knows, but he has surely been around as long as the human mind. This wily and slippery conjurer deludes us into believing that we can only enjoy the delights of the senses without pain by delivering ourselves into his hands.

Of the many devices employed by Ego to keep us in his

power, none is more effective than language. The English language is so structured that it demands the repeated use of the personal pronoun "I" for grammatical nicety and presumed clarity. Actually this I is no more than a figure of speech, a convenient convention, but we talk and act as though it were real and true. Listen to any conversation and see how the stress invariably falls on the "I"—"I said . . ." "I did . . ." "I like . . ." "I hate . . ." All this plays into the hands of Ego, strengthening our servitude and enlarging our sufferings, for the more we postulate this I the more we are exposed to Ego's never-ending demands.

We cannot evade responsibility for this state of affairs by claiming ignorance, for the machinations of Ego, as well as the way to be free of them, have been pointed out time and again by the wisest of men. After all, language is our creation. It reflects our values, ideals, and goals, and the way we see and relate to the world. There are languages that do not insist on the constant repetition of the vertical pronoun for clarity or grammatical completeness. In Japanese, for example, it is possible to make sentences without the "I" or other personal pronouns in all but a few cases. The Japanese ideal of personal behavior, which the language reflects, is modesty and self-effacement, in theory at least if not always in practice. The strong assertion of the Ego-I in contemporary American speech, as well as the decline of the passive voice in favor of the active, shows that we no longer value humility and self-effacement, if we ever did.

Our relative mind of Ego, aided by language, deceives us

in other ways. It constantly tempts us into distinctions and judgments that take us farther and farther from the concrete and the real into the realm of the speculative and the abstract. Take the case of an individual walking alone who suddenly hears the sound of a bell. Immediately his discriminating mind evaluates it as beautiful or weird, or distinguishes it as a church bell or some other kind. Ideas associated with a similar sound heard in the past may also intrude upon the mind, and these are analyzed and compared. With each such judgment the experience of pure hearing becomes fainter and fainter until one no longer hears the sound but hears only his *thoughts* about it.

Or again, we tacitly agree among ourselves to call a certain object a "tree." We then forget that "tree" is an arbitrary concept which in no way reveals the true identity of this object. What, then, is a tree? A philosopher might call it ultimate truth; a botanist, a living organism; a physicist, a mass of protons and neutrons swirling around a nucleus; an artist, a unique shape with distinctive coloring; a carpenter, a potential table. To a dog, however, it is nothing but a urinal. All descriptions, explanations or analyses are but a looking from one side at that which has infinite dimensions. The true nature of the tree is more than anything that can be said about it.

Similarly, we tinker with time by dividing it into past, present, and future and into years, months, days, etc. This is convenient, but we need to remember that this "slicing" is artificial and arbitrary, the product of our discriminating mind, which discerns only the surface of things. Timelessness is un-accounted for. Thus, we conceive a world that is conceptual, limited, and far removed from the actual.

Speaking of the way in which language falsifies reality, Korzybski, the father of general semantics, points the accusing finger at the verb "to be" as the chief offender. "The difficulty with the verb 'to be,' " Korzybski is quoted as saying, "is that it implies a static, absolute quality, whereas the law of the universe is constant change. The moment one says, 'This rose is red' it has already changed into something else. Besides, to someone else the rose may appear to be pink. Better to say," adds Korzybski, " 'This rose appears to me as red.' " For Zen, however, a rose is not merely red, pink, yellow, but it is all colors and at the same time it is *no* color. Does not a "Rose is a rose is a rose" more nearly convey the cosmic grandeur and infinite beauty of a rose than "This rose appears to me as red"? But why say anything? Enter the heart of the rose—smell it, touch it, taste it—and what is there to say except perhaps, "Ah, wonderful!" or better yet, simply, "Ah!" or best of all, just a smile—a smile that flowers.

The Zen masters have always been alert to the snare of language, which "fits over experience like a glove," and have used language in such ways as to liberate their disciples from its bind. What are these methods? Hui-neng, the Sixth Patri-arch, once taught: "If somebody asks you a question expecting 'Yes' for an answer, answer 'No,' and vice versa. If he asks you about an ordinary man, answer as if he asked about a saint, and vice versa. By this use of relatives teach him the doctrine of the Mean. Answer all his questions in this fashion and you will not fall into error."

Chao-Chou (Jōshu in Japanese), a famous Zen master, was frequently asked, "Is it true that even a dog has the Buddha-nature?" the implication of the question being that if such an exalted being as man has the pure, all-embracing Buddha-nature, how can such a lowly creature as a dog also have it? To this question Chao-Chou sometimes answered, "No, it hasn't" (*Mū* in Japanese, *Wu* in Chinese), and at other times, "Yes, it has." The questioners may have been genuinely puzzled by the statement in the sutras to the effect that all beings possess the Buddha-nature, or they may have been feigning ignorance in order to see how Chao-Chou would respond. Since Buddha-nature is common to all existence, logically either answer makes no sense. But more than logic is involved here. So what is Chao-Chou up to? Is he flouting the logic of language to show the monks that absolute truth lies beyond affirmation and negation, or is he, by the manner in which he utters "Yes!" or "No!" actually thrusting this Buddha-nature at his questioners?

In another well-known episode Nan-Chüan, the teacher of Chao-Chou, returned to his monastery one day to find some of his monks quarreling about a cat sitting in front of them. Presumably they were arguing about whether a cat, like a dog, also has the Buddha-nature. Sizing up the situation at once and taking advantage of the occasion to bring home to them the truth they were obscuring, Nan-Chüan suddenly seized the cat, held it aloft and demanded, "One of you monks, give me a word of Zen! If you can I will spare the life of the cat, otherwise I will cut it in two!" No one knew what to say, so Nan-Chüan boldly cut the cat in two (not really, though; he merely went through the motions of doing so; "cutting the cat" makes the episode more vivid and dramatic). That evening Chao-Chou, who had also been away, returned. Nan-Chüan told him what had happened and asked, "Suppose you had been there. What would you have done?" Without a word Chao-Chou took off his slippers, placed them on his head, and slowly walked out of the room. "If only you had been there," said Nan-Chüan admiringly, "you would have saved the life of the cat."

Now what is a word of Zen? In Zen there are what are called live words and dead ones. The admired live word is the gut word, concrete and vibrant with feeling; the dead word is the explanatory word, dry and lifeless, issuing from the head. The first unifies; the second separates and divides. Neither the monks nor Chao-Chou spoke a word, yet Nan-Chüan put down the monks and praised Chao-Chou. Why? What was the significance of Chao-Chou's putting his slippers on his head and walking out? What did Nan-Chüan demonstrate by his act of "cutting" the cat in two? And say where that dead cat is right now! Aren't we all dead cats whenever we argue and speculate, make gratuitous assumptions, jump to conclusions?

A Chinese Zen master once gave this problem to his disciples: "A monk is hanging by his teeth from a branch high up in a tree. His hands can't reach a branch above him nor his

feet touch a branch underneath. On the ground below someone seriously asks, 'What is the highest truth of Buddhism?' If
he opens his mouth to speak he will fall down and possibly be
killed. Yet if he doesn't respond he evades his duty. What
should he do?"

This is not a teaser designed to titillate the intellect—far
from it. Among other things, it points up a fundamental problem in human relations: when to speak and when to remain
silent. For to spin fine words and empty phrases, to embroider
theories and explanations of one kind or another can be harm-
ful, even fatal, to one's personality. But to be silent and not
speak when by so doing we can help a suffering fellow being
is craven. Also, there are many forms of silence. There is the
silence where one doesn't know what to say, the silence which
is the better part of valor, and the silence which speaks louder
than words. Which of these forms of silence was the monk's,
and furthermore, was he answering the question put to him or
not?

These episodes or teaching methods were collected by
later generations of masters and given to their students to
solve as part of their training. They came to be called *koan*
(*kung-an* in Chinese; literally "a public record"); that is, cases
that could be relied upon as pointing to and embodying ultimate truth. They are not unlike cases of common law that
establish legal precedent. One of the prizes of *Zen Keys* is a
series of forty-three koan, appearing in English for the first
time, by Tran Thai Tong, a Vietnamese who was the first king
of the Tran Dynasty (1225–1400) in Vietnam. He practiced

Zen while still reigning, and at the age of forty-one gave up his throne to his son, devoting himself thereafter to the most intensive practice of Zen. Each of the koan contains a theme, a brief commentary and a verse, all by Tran Thai Tong. Though in the style of the *Mumonkan,* a well-known Chinese book of koan, they nonetheless have a flavor distinctly their own.

Chapter VI of *Zen Keys,* entitled "The Regeneration of Humanity," may strike sophisticated readers as naïve and perhaps even simplistic. Yet it would be a mistake to pass over lightly what lies behind the simple expression. Among other things, Thich Nhat Hanh pleads for a dialogue between East and West based upon mutual respect and understanding and not on feelings of Western superiority. These sentiments have been echoed innumerable times by thoughtful and knowledgeable Asians. We in the West must heed this wise and earnest voice speaking out of the heart of Asia if we are to avoid a third world war and the not improbable destruction of most of the human race and our planet earth. Americans especially must listen with an unprejudiced, believing heart, for not only is our karma with Vietnam and Asia deep—in one generation we have fought three land wars there—but to a large extent the fate of humanity rests upon us. To all but the obtuse it is clear that the world is at a crossroads, its very survival at stake.

We need to recover our basic humanity. Pride in our technological achievements has replaced love of our fellows, as Nhat Hanh observes. We need to purge ourselves of pride and self-seeking. Above all, we must regenerate ourselves morally and awaken spiritually, and this means becoming aware of the true nature of things and of our responsibilities to the world. The contamination of our own and the world's environment and our squandering of dwindling natural resources through overconsumption, waste, and mismanagement speak eloquently of our greed and irresponsibility. How long will the rest of the world stand by while we in America with only about 5 percent of the world's population consume nearly 40 percent of its resources? The global crisis we are now experiencing may well be the first signal of the revolt against this intolerable situation.

Many in America are beginning to understand this, and even our government leaders are saying we must drastically alter our style of living. Do they really understand the spiritual implications of this? How are we to uproot the greed, anger, and wrong thinking lying at the base of our actions? How, in other words, are we to horizontalize the mast of the inflated national ego?

One obvious answer is—through Zen. Not necessarily Zen Buddhism but Zen in its broad sense of a one-pointed aware mind; of a disciplined life of simplicity and naturalness as against a contrived and artificial one; of a life compassionately concerned with our own and the world's welfare and not self-centered and aggressive. A life, in short, of harmony with the natural order of things and not in constant conflict with it.

The problems of pollution that we hear so much about have always been dealt with in Zen training. Zen, after all, speaks to the most fundamental pollution of all, the pollution of the human mind. Additionally, we have never been without an energy crisis either. This energy crisis is an internal one: how to mobilize the unlimited energy locked within us—how to split the atom of the mind if you like—and use it wisely for ourselves and mankind. For it is the release of this energy that leads to awakening and Awareness, not only of body and mind, but of the planet as well.

As *Zen Keys* points out, in the East, Zen is declining due to war and the heavy inroads of materialism and technology. In the West, however, it is the disenchantment with the "good" life produced by materialism and technology that is largely fueling the current interest in Zen. For together with the realization that technology makes "major contributions to minor needs of man" is the awareness that we have become cogs in an out-of-control wheel, living by a value system that does not see man as a human being but merely as a consumer of things. If Zen is to find a permanent home in the West and become a living force in the lives of Europeans and Americans, it is obvious it will have to shed its Eastern cultural accretions and develop new forms in response to the needs of our own culture and society. This Thich Nhat Hanh and other Zen-oriented Asians affirm.

The outline of the new Western Zen is already emerging. It is away from a monastic-based Zen and more in the direction of large centers where ordained men and women and laypeople practice the Buddha's way together, with smaller affiliated communities functioning in other areas of the country. We also find many of the more "aware" trends in American society being incorporated into the lifestyle of these Zen communities. Many of these groups are eating natural foods, gardening organically, and living communally, as well as including within their Zen training such body-mind disciplines as *hatha* yoga and *tai-chi chuan*. In their religious life as well, they are beginning to create meaningful ceremonies and rituals appropriate to Westerners. Also, in some cities members of Zen communities, carrying burlap bags, periodically clean up their neighborhoods, thereby learning humility and non-attachment. Others take such menial jobs as housecleaners, dishwashers, and garbage men for the same reasons. Their lives truly reflect the principle that "a man is rich, not in what he possesses but in what he can do without with dignity."

It would be a great pity, though, if Western Zen severed its links with the great Asian traditions that spawned and nourished it; this would in effect be discarding hundreds of years of experiential knowledge of the human mind. Always there is the danger of throwing out the baby with the bathwater.

As the first authoritative book in English on the Zen Buddhist tradition of Vietnam, *Zen Keys* is one more bright link in the chain of Asian Zen and for this reason invaluable.

Though originally written in the early 1970s, this is by no means only representative of the needs and questions of that era. Those who are interested in Buddhism will find it at least as useful today. There are, however, ways in which Thich Nhat Hanh has learned over his past twenty years of teaching and practice, and he has made thorough revisions in keeping with this broader experience. Now as much as when it was first published, *Zen Keys* conveys the authentic "feel" and flavor of Zen. Understandably so, for it is a loving and knowledgeable work.

PHILIP KAPLEAU
Hollywood, Florida

I

THE PRACTICE OF

MINDFULNESS

THE LITTLE BOOK

I entered Tu Hiêu Zen Monastery in the Imperial City of Hué when I was sixteen years old. After a brief adjustment to monastic life, I presented myself before the monk responsible for my training and asked him to teach me the Zen "way." He gave me a small book, *The Little Manual of Practice*, printed in Chinese characters, and asked me to learn it by heart.

I thanked him and went to my room to study. This book —which is famous in Zen circles—is divided into three parts: 1) "Practice in Everyday Life"; 2) "Essential Practices for a Novice"; and 3) "The Teachings of Zen Master Kuai Chan." There is no philosophy at all in this book. All three parts discuss only practical problems. The first part teaches how to calm and concentrate the mind. The second discusses the precepts and other practices essential to monastic life. The third is a beautiful exhortation to Zen students to encourage them to remember that their time and life are precious and should not be vainly dissipated. I was assured that not only young novices begin with this book, but that monks even forty and fifty also followed its prescriptions.

Before entering the monastery, I had already received some Western education, and I had the impression that the methods of teaching Buddhism in the monasteries were a little old-fashioned. First we were asked to learn the whole book by heart. Then we were to begin practicing without even being given the theoretical principles underlying it. I shared these concerns with another novice, who told me, "This is the way followed here. If you want to learn Zen, you must accept it." So I resigned myself to beginning my practice in the traditional way.

The first part of The Little Manual, "Practice in Everyday Life," contains gathas, short verses that bring the energy of mindfulness to each act of daily life. For example, when I wash my hands, I bring forth this thought: "Water flows over these hands. May I use them skillfully to preserve our precious planet." When I am sitting in the meditation hall, I think: "Sitting here is like sitting under the bodhi tree. My body is mindfulness itself, entirely free from distraction." And even when using the toilet, I say to myself: "Defiled or immaculate, increasing or decreasing—these concepts exist only in our minds. The reality of interbeing is unsurpassed."

"Practice in Everyday Life" contains a total of fifty gathas. We have to practice intelligently so that we can compose others when we need them. The ones in the manual are only examples. We should modify or even change them and write others more suited to our needs and contemporary conditions. Suppose I am about to use the telephone. There is no gatha for using the telephone in The Little Manual, because at the time the book was written there were no telephones. I have invented a number of gathas, like the following: "Words can travel thousands of miles. May my words create mutual under-standing and love. May they be beautiful as gems, as lovely as flowers." I have compiled a book of traditional and modern gathas entitled *Present Moment Wonderful Moment: Mindfulness Verses for Daily Living*, for your use in the practice.

When I was sixteen, I thought *The Little Manual* was written for young people and those just beginning the practice of Zen. I thought this method was just for preparation. But to-day, more than fifty years later, I know that *The Little Manual* is the very essence of Zen Buddhism.

NECESSARY AWARENESS

I remember a short conversation between the Buddha and a philosopher of his time.

"I have heard that Buddhism is a doctrine of enlighten-ment. What is your method? What do you practice every day?"

"We walk, we eat, we wash ourselves, we sit down . . ."

"What is so special about that? Everyone walks, eats, washes, sits down . . ."

"Sir, when we walk, we are aware that we are walking; when we eat, we are aware that we are eating. . . . When others walk, eat, wash, or sit down, they are generally not aware of what they are doing."

In Buddhism, mindfulness is the key. Mindfulness is the

energy that sheds light on all things and all activities, producing the power of concentration, bringing forth deep insight
and awakening. Mindfulness is at the base of all Buddhist practice.

   To shed light on all things? This is the point of departure. If I
live without mindfulness, in forgetfulness, I am, as Albert
Camus says in his novel *The Stranger,* living "like a dead person." The ancient Zen masters used to say, "If we live in forgetfulness, we die in a dream." How many among us live "like
a dead person"! The first thing we have to do is to return to
life, to wake up and be mindful of each thing we do. Are we
aware when we are eating, drinking, sitting in meditation? Or
are we wasting our time, living in forgetfulness?

   To produce the power of concentration? Mindfulness helps us
focus our attention on and know what we are doing. Usually
we are a prisoner of society. Our energies are dispersed here
and there. Our body and our mind are not in harmony. To
begin to be aware of what we are doing, saying, and thinking
is to begin to resist the invasion by our surroundings and by
all of our wrong perceptions. When the lamp of awareness is
lit, our whole being lights up, and each passing thought and
emotion is also lit up. Self-confidence is reestablished, the
shadows of illusion no longer overwhelm us, and our concentration develops to its fullest. We wash our hands, dress, per-
form everyday actions as before, but now we are *aware* of our
actions, words, and thoughts.

The practice of mindfulness is not only for novices. It is a lifelong practice for everyone, even the Buddha himself. The power of mindfulness and concentration is the spiritual force behind all of the great men and women of human history.

To bring forth deep insight and awakening? The aim of Zen Buddhism is a clear vision of reality, seeing things as they are, and that is acquired by the power of concentration. This clear vision is enlightenment. Enlightenment is always enlightenment about something. It is not abstract.

MINDFULNESS

This process—to *shed light on all things,* to *produce the power of concentration,* and to *bring forth deep insight and awakening*—is called in Buddhism the "Threefold Training": *Sila* (precepts), *samadhi* (concentration), and *prajña* (insight). The word "sila" also means mindfulness, because the essence of the precepts is mindfulness. Precepts in Buddhism are not imposed by some outside authority. They arise from our own insight based on the practice of mindfulness. To be attached to the form without understanding the essence is to fall into what Buddhism calls *attachment to rules.* We realize insight by practicing mindfulness of our body, feelings, mind, and the objects of our mind, which are the world. That is why the first part of *The*

Little Manual consists of mindfulness verses to memorize, and is
called "Practice in Everyday Life."

When a scientist works in her laboratory, she does not
smoke, eat sweets, or listen to the radio. The scientist refrains
from doing these things not because they are immoral, but
because she knows that they impede perfect concentration on
the object of her study. It is the same in Zen. The precepts
help us live in mindfulness.

In Zen, insight cannot be obtained just by the intellect—
study, hypothesis, analysis, synthesis. The Zen student must
use his or her entire being as an instrument of realization; the
intellect is only one part of our being, and a part that often
pulls us away from living reality, which is the very substance
of Zen. That is why *The Little Manual* does not present Buddhism as a theory—it introduces the practitioner directly into
the daily practice of Zen.

In the monastery, the practitioner does everything in
mindfulness: carries water, looks for firewood, prepares food,
plants lettuce. . . . Although we learn to meditate in the sitting position, we also learn to be mindful while carrying water, cooking, or planting lettuce. We know that to carry water
is not merely a utilitarian action, it is the very essence of Zen.
If we do not practice while carrying water, it is a waste of time
to seclude ourselves in a monastery. But if we are mindful of
each thing we do, even if we do the exact same things as
others, we can enter directly into the world of Zen.

A Zen master observes the student in silence, while the
student tries to bring the practice into every moment of life.

The student may feel that he is not receiving enough attention, but his ways and acts cannot escape the observation of the master. The master can see if the student is or is not "awake." If, for example, the student shuts the door noisily or carelessly, he is demonstrating a lack of mindfulness. Closing the door gently is not in itself a virtuous act, but awareness of the fact that you are closing the door is an expression of real practice. In this case, the master simply reminds the student to close the door gently, to be mindful. The master does this not only to respect the quiet of the monastery, but to point out to the student that he was not practicing mindfulness, that his acts were not majestic or subtle. It is said in Buddhism that there are ninety thousand "subtle gestures" to practice. These gestures and acts are expressions of the presence of mindfulness. All that we say, think, and do in mindfulness are described as having "the flavor of Zen."

If a practitioner hears himself reproached for lacking the "flavor of Zen" in what he says and does, he should recognize that he is being reminded to live his life in mindfulness.

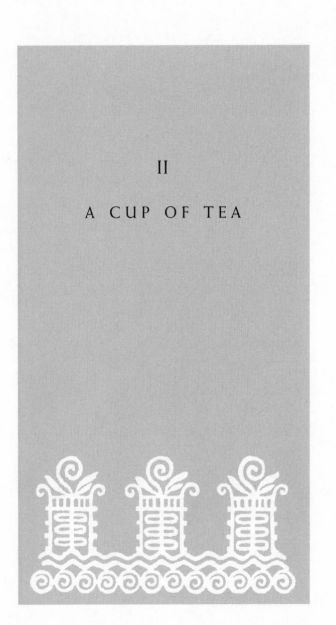

II

A CUP OF TEA

Seeing into One's Own Nature

In all Zen temples, there are fine portraits of Bodhidharma. The one in my monastery was a Chinese work in ink, depicting the Indian monk with intense, vigorous features. His eyebrows, eyes, and chin express a determined spirit. Bodhidharma lived, it is said, in the fifth century, and is considered to be the First Ancestral Teacher of Zen Buddhism in China. It might be that many of the things reported about his life are not valid historically, but the personality and mind of this monk, as described through the tradition, have made him the ideal person for all who aspire to Zen enlightenment.

His is the picture of someone who has attained perfect self-mastery, complete freedom, and tremendous spiritual power that allow him to regard happiness, unhappiness, and all vicissitudes of life with absolute calmness and clarity. The essence of his personality does not come from a position taken about the problem of absolute reality nor from an indomitable will, but from a deep insight into his own mind and all living reality. The Zen phrase used is "seeing into one's own nature." When one has reached this enlightenment, one sees all wrong views dissolve within oneself. A new vision that produces deep peace, great tranquillity, and a spiritual strength characterized

by the absence of fear is born. *Seeing into one's own nature* is the
goal of Zen.

BODHIDHARMA'S STATEMENT

Seeing into one's own nature is not the fruit of study or research. It is a profound insight derived from living in the heart
of reality, in perfect mindfulness. According to Bodhidharma,
Zen is:

> a special transmission outside the scriptures, not based
> on words or letters, a direct pointing to the heart of
> reality so that we might see into our own nature and
> wake up.

In the fifth century, when Bodhidharma came to China,
Chinese Buddhists were studying Buddhist texts that had re-
cently been translated. They were occupied more with sys-
tematizing the ideas and forming Buddhist sects than with
practicing meditation. Bodhidharma's statement was like a
thunder clap to wake them up and bring them to the practice
and the experiential spirit of Buddhism.

Because it is like thunder, Bodhidharma's statement may
seem extreme. But if we examine the relationship between Zen
and Indian Buddhism, we see that Bodhidharma's pronounce-

ment is very much in the same spirit as the teaching of the
Buddha.

Bodhidharma said:

Zen has been transmitted directly by the Buddha and
has nothing at all to do with the scriptures and doctrines you are studying.

At first glance, it may seem that Zen is a kind of secret
teaching transmitted from master to disciple, not passed on by
writing or comment—a spiritual heritage that only initiates
can understand. One could not even talk about teaching it,
since Zen cannot be taught through symbols; it passes directly
from master to student, from "mind to mind." The image often
used is a *seal* imprinted on the mind, not of wood, copper, or
ivory, but a "mind seal." The word "transmission" denotes the
transmission of this mind seal. Zen itself *is* a mind seal. The
enormous canon of Buddhist scriptures might be of Buddhism,
but not of Zen Buddhism. Zen is not found in the scriptures,
because Zen "is not based on words or letters." This interpre-
tation is often given to Bodhidharma's dictum by commenta-
tors.

This misunderstanding occurs because these commenta-
tors overlook the intimate ties between Zen and early Buddhism. The frowning upon describing ultimate reality by
words is common to all teachings of the Buddha. Bodhidharma's statement is very much in this tradition and is

merely a drastic way to bring people to a *direct spiritual experience*.

THE BUDDHIST REVOLUTION

Buddhism was born toward the end of the sixth century B.C.E. The word "Buddhism" comes from the Sanskrit verb *Budh*, which in the Vedic scriptures foremostly signifies "to know," then "to wake up." The one who *knows*, the one who *wakes up*, is called a buddha. The Chinese have translated the word "buddha" as "an awakened person." *Buddhism is, therefore, a doctrine of awakening, a doctrine of insight and understanding.*

But the Buddha made it known from the beginning that this awakening, this understanding, can only be acquired by the practice of the "Way" and not by studies or speculation. Liberation, in Buddhism, comes about through understanding and not by grace or merit.

The rise of Buddhism in India must be considered a new vision of humanity and life. This vision was expounded first as a reaction against the Brahmanic practices and beliefs that dominated the society of the time. What was this society? From the intellectual standpoint, the authority of the Brahmanic tradition dominated all: the Vedic revelation, the divine supremacy of Brahma, and the miraculous power of sacrifice were the three fundamentals one could not dispute. From the standpoint of belief, Brahma, Vishnu, and Shiva were the object of all the schools. From the philosophical standpoint, the thoughts of the Vedas and Upanishads were the basis of all philosophical concepts. Sankhya, Yoga, and the six philosophical schools were born and developed on this basis. Buddhism was thoroughly opposed to absolute Vedic authority and to all the points of view stemming from it. From the standpoint of belief, Buddhism rejected all deisms and all forms of sacrifice. From the social point of view, Buddhism combated the caste system, accepting untouchables in the order at the same level as a king. (Buddha, having met an untouchable who carried night soil, brought him to the edge of the river to wash him, then accepted him into the Buddhist community, despite the extreme protests of the others.) From the intellectual standpoint, it rigorously rejected the notion of a Self (*Atman*), which is the very heart of Brahmanism.

One can see how Buddha reacted against the currents of thought of his time by reading, for example, the *Brahmajalasutta*, which is found in the *Dighanikaya (Long Discourses)*. His opposition to Brahmanic thought must be regarded primarily as a reaction, a revolt, rather than as an effort to present the Buddhist point of view. It does not mean that all the thoughts contained in the Vedas and Upanishads are erroneous or contrary to truth. This opposition is a clap of thunder aimed at giving a great shock in order to change the customs, manners, and modes of thought that had brought society to an impasse.

Because Brahmanism considers the concept of Atman (Self) as a basis for its methodology and its ontology, Buddha posited the doctrine of the *Anatman* (not-self). What did he mean? *This self of which you speak, whether it is the great self or the small self, is only a concept that does not correspond to any reality.*

If we think in ontological terms, we might say the doctrine of not-self was considered by the Buddha as a truth opposing the doctrine of self, but this is not corrrect. If we think in methodological terms, we see immediately that the notion of not-self is an antidote aimed at liberating us from the prison of dogma. Before examining the question of truth and falsehood, it is necessary to examine the attitudes and methods. This allows us to say that the notion of not-self was born in reaction to the Brahmanic notion of the self, and not as a discovery independent of the thought of the time. It was a simple reaction that later served as the point of departure for a new understanding.

NOT-SELF

Drastic methods are frequently used in Buddhism to uproot habits and prejudices. This characteristic trait of Buddhism is manifested most energetically in Zen.

The Buddha used the notion of the not-self to upset and to destroy. Later, he used it to expound his teaching of awakening. It can thus be said that the notion of not-self is the point of departure of Buddhism.

Buddhist scriptures often speak of the "not-self" nature of all phenomena. Things do not possess a self (*Sarva dharmas nairatmya*). Nothing in itself contains an absolute identity. This means a rejection of the principle of identity, which is the basis of formal logic. According to this principle, A must be A, B must be B, and A cannot be B. The doctrine of not-self says: A is not A, B is not B, and A can be B. This is something that shocks people and invites them to reexamine themselves.

In order to understand not-self, the concept of impermanence (*anitya*) in Buddhism must also be considered. All is impermanent. Everything is in a state of perpetual change. Nothing remains the same for two consecutive *ksanas* (the shortest imaginable periods of time). It is because things transform themselves ceaselessly that they cannot maintain their identity, even during two consecutive ksanas. Not being able to fix their identity, they are not-self; that is to say, devoid of absolute identity. Not having a fixed identity, A is no longer the A of the preceding ksana; this is why one says that A is not A. Impermanence is another name for not-self. In time, things are impermanent; in space they are devoid of a fixed identity. Not only are physical phenomena impermanent and without a separate self, but the same is true of physiological phenomena, for example our body, mental phenomena, and feelings.

Many people think that anatman and anitya are the basis for a pessimistic moral doctrine. They say, "If all things are impermanent and devoid of a fixed identity, why bother to struggle so hard to obtain them?" This is a misunderstanding of the Buddha's teaching. Buddhism aims at liberation through understanding. It is therefore necessary to examine the teachings of the Buddha from the point of view of understanding, and not to take his words too literally without understanding their meaning. Impermanence and not-self are important principles that lead to deep understanding.

THINGS AND CONCEPTS

The principle of not-self brings to light the gap between things themselves and the concepts we have of them. Things are dynamic and alive, while our concepts are static. Look, for example, at a table. We have the impression that the table itself and our concept of it are identical. In reality, what we believe to be a table is only our concept. The table itself is quite different. Some notions—wood, brown, hard, three feet high, old, etc.—give rise to a concept of table in us. The table itself is always more than that. For example, a nuclear physicist will tell us that the table is a multitude of atoms whose electrons are moving like a swarm of bees, and that if we could put these atoms next to each other, the mass of matter would be smaller than one finger. This *table*, in reality, is always in transformation; in time as well as in space it is made only of *non-table* elements. It depends on these elements so much that if we were to remove them from the table, there would be nothing left.

The forest, the tree, the saw, the hammer, and the cabinetmaker are non-table elements, as are the parents of the cabinetmaker, the bread that they eat, the blacksmith who makes the hammer, and so on. If we know how to look deeply at the table, we can see the presence of all these non-table elements in it. The existence of the table demonstrates the existence of all non-table elements, in fact, of the entire universe. This idea is expressed in the Avatamsaka system of Buddhism by the notion of interbeing.

THE INTERBEING OF THINGS

Genesis in Buddhism is called interbeing. The birth, growth, and decline of things depend upon multiple causes and conditions and not just a single one. The presence of one thing (*dharma*) implies the presence of all other things. The enlightened man or woman sees each thing not as a separate entity but as a complete manifestation of reality. The twelfth-century Vietnamese Zen monk, Dao Hanh, said, "If one thing exists, everything exists, even a speck of dust. If one thing is empty, everything is empty, even the whole universe."

The doctrine of not-self aims at bringing to light the *interbeing nature of things;* and, at the same time, demonstrates to us that the concepts we have of things do not reflect and cannot convey reality. The world of concepts is not the world of reality. Conceptual knowledge is not the perfect instrument for studying truth. Words are inadequate to express the truth of ultimate reality.

THE VANITY OF METAPHYSICS

These preliminary remarks are the point of departure of Zen Buddhism. If concepts do not represent reality, then conceptual knowledge of reality can be considered erroneous. That is demonstrated many times in Buddhism. The Buddha always told his disciples not to waste their time and energy in metaphysical speculation. Whenever he was asked a metaphysical question, he remained silent. Instead, he directed his disciples toward practical efforts. Questioned one day about the problem of the infinity of the world, the Buddha said, "Whether the world is finite or infinite, limited or unlimited, the problem of your liberation remains the same." Another time he said, "Suppose a man is struck by a poisoned arrow and the doctor wishes to take out the arrow immediately. Suppose the man does not want the arrow removed until he knows who shot it, his age, his parents, and why he shot it. What would happen? If he were to wait until all these questions have been answered, the man might die first." Life is so short. It must not be spent in endless metaphysical speculation that does not bring us any closer to the truth.

But if conceptual knowledge is fallible, what other instrument should we use to grasp reality? According to Buddhism, we only reach reality through direct experience. Study and speculation are based on concepts. In conceptualizing we cut reality into small pieces that seem to be independent of one another. This manner of conceiving things is called *imaginative*

and discriminative knowledge (vikalpa) according to the Vijñanavadin school of Buddhism. The faculty that directly experiences
reality without passing through concepts is called *non-discriminative and non-imaginative wisdom (nirvikalpajñana).* This wisdom is
the fruit of meditation. It is a direct and perfect knowledge of
reality, a form of understanding in which one does not distinguish between subject and object. It cannot be conceived by
the intellect nor expressed by language.

EXPERIENCE ITSELF

Suppose I invite you to join me for a cup of tea. You receive
your cup, taste the tea, and then drink a little more. You seem
to be enjoying it. Then you put your cup on the table and we
have a conversation.

Now, suppose I ask you to describe the tea. You use your
memory, your concepts, and your vocabulary to describe the
sensations. You may say, "It is very good tea, the best Tieh
Kuan Ying tea, manufactured in Taipei. I can still taste it in my
mouth. It is very refreshing." You could express your sensation
in many other ways. But these concepts and these words *de-
scribe* your *direct experience* of the tea; *they are not the experience itself.*
Indeed, in the direct experience of the tea, you do not make
the distinction that you are the subject of the experience and
that the tea is its object; you do not think that the tea is the
best, or the worst, of the Tieh Kuan Ying of Taipei. There is

no concept or word that can frame this pure sensation result-
ing from experience. You can offer as many descriptions as
you like, but only you have had a direct experience of the tea.
When someone listens to you, she can re-create for herself
certain sensations, based on experiences that she might have
had, but that is all. And you yourself, when you are describing
the experience, are already no longer in it. In the experience,
you were one with the tea. There was no distinction between
subject and object, no evaluation, and no discrimination. That
pure sensation is an example of *non-discriminative wisdom*, which
introduces us to the heart of reality.

THE MOMENT OF AWAKENING

To reach truth is not to accumulate knowledge, but to awaken
to the *heart of reality*. Reality reveals itself complete and whole
at the moment of awakening. In the light of awakening, nothing is added and nothing is lost. Emotions based on concepts
no longer affect us. If Bodhidharma is an ideal person, it is
because he has broken the chains of illusion that bind us to
the world of concepts. The hammer used to break these chains
is the practice of Zen. The moment of awakening may be
marked by an outburst of laughter, but this is not the laughter
of someone who has won the lottery or some kind of victory.
It is the laughter of one who, after searching for something for
a long time, suddenly finds it in the pocket of his coat.

One day the Buddha was standing in front of the assembly at Vulture Peak. Everyone was waiting for him to begin his Dharma talk, but he remained silent. After a long time, he held up a flower, still not uttering a single word. Everyone in the assembly looked at him, but they did not understand at all. Then one monk looked at the Buddha with sparkling eyes and smiled. The Buddha said, "I have the treasure of the vision of the perfect Dharma, the marvelous spirit of *nirvana*, the reality without impurity, and I have transmitted them to Mahakasyapa." The monk who smiled was, indeed, Mahakasyapa, one of the great disciples of the Buddha.

Mahakasyapa reached the moment of awakening when Buddha raised his flower. He truly saw the flower, and he received the "mind seal" of the Buddha, to use the Zen terminology. Buddha had transmitted his deep understanding from mind to mind. He had taken the seal of his mind and imprinted it on the mind of Mahakasyapa. The smile of Mahakasyapa was not a great outburst, but it was of the exact same nature and quality as the outbursts of laughter of the great Zen masters. Mahakasyapa arrived at awakening thanks to the flower and to his deep looking. Some Zen masters have attained awakening through a shout, a cry, or even a kick.

III

THE CYPRESS IN THE
COURTYARD

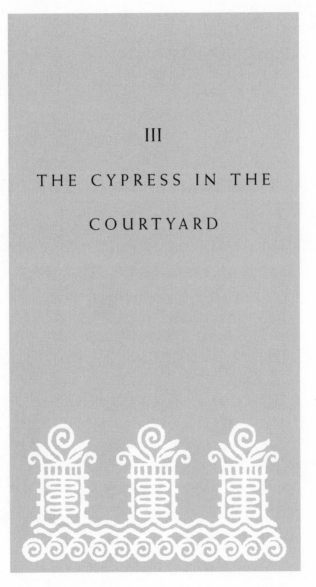

The Language of Zen

The essence of Zen is awakening. This is why *one does not talk about Zen, one experiences it.* But awakening is a great phenomenon that radiates like the sun. The "awakened" person is recognizable by particular signs. First of all is liberty; he does not allow himself to be tossed about by the vicissitudes of life, by fear, joy, anxiety, success, or failure. Then there is the spiritual force that reveals itself in calmness, an ineffable smile, and deep serenity. The smile, the look, the word, and the action of the awakened person constitute the *language* of awakening. This language is used by Zen masters to guide practitioners. A Zen master uses words and concepts like everyone else, but he is neither conditioned nor captivated by these words or concepts. The language of Zen always aims at destroying the habit-energies of those who only know how to think conceptually. It tends to provoke crises, whose function it is to bring to fruition the precious moment of awakening.

Let us examine fragments of two conversations:

(1) Chao-Chou: What is the Way?
    Nan-Chüan: It is our everyday mind.
    Chao-Chou: Is it necessary to realize it?

Nan-Chüan: To intend to realize the Way is
              opposed to the Way.

Chao-Chou: Without intending, how can you
              know whether it is the Way?

Nan-Chüan: The Way does not depend on
              what you know or do not know.
              If you know it, your knowledge is
              just speculative ideas. If you
              don't, your ignorance is like the
              inanimate. When you have no
              doubts, the unlimited universe
              will open in front of you, and no
              discrimination is possible.

(2) A monk asks Zen master Chao-Chou: What
    was Bodhidharma's intention in coming to
    China?

Chao-Chou: Look at the cypress in the
              courtyard.

The first dialogue shows the obstacles created by conceptualizing and engages the questioner in the way of non-discriminative realization. The second conversation shakes loose
the habit of conceptualization and creates the shock required
to bring about awakening. If the mind of the student is ripe,
enlightenment can occur right away.

An awakened Zen master understands his or her students
and can offer ways to help them enter the world of awakening.
The language of Zen is one of these ways. It must:

1. possess the power of liberating us from prejudices and attachments to knowledge;
2. be suitable to the person to whom it is addressed; and
3. be skillful and effective.

THE FINGER AND THE MOON

As reality can only be lived and experienced, Buddhist teachings never attempt to describe reality. They only serve as methods to guide practitioners in the direction of reality.

"The Perfect Awakening *Sutra*" (*Mahavaipulyapurnabuddha Sutra*) says: "All of the Buddha's teachings are a finger pointing to the moon." To see the moon, we use the finger, but we must not mix up the finger and the moon. The finger is not the moon. "Skillful means"—in Sanskrit, *upaya*—are methods created to guide people toward awakening. But if these methods are taken as a description of awakening or as awakening itself, they become a kind of prison. *As soon as we think that the finger is the moon, we will no longer look in the direction the finger is pointing.*

Skillful means can be a verbal declaration or a simple gesture. Great masters possess what Buddhism calls the *Wisdom of the Skillful Ways (upaya-jñana),* or the capacity to create and employ different methods suitable for different personalities and different occasions. The conversations between Chao-

Chou and Nan-Chüan, for example, are skillful means. The cypress in the courtyard and the flower held by Buddha are also skillful means.

But these means are only skillful if they are suitable to the *particular circumstances*. For them to be *effective*, they must fulfill the real needs and the particular mentalities of those they seek to guide. If a master is not capable of understanding the mentality of the student, he or she will not be able to create skillful or effective means. No single means is suitable for all circumstances. Teachers must create new means all the time by relying on their understanding of the Buddha's way and their understanding of their students and the circumstances. Buddhism speaks of the 84,000 Dharma doors, entrances to reality. Zen underlines the importance of effectiveness and skillfulness in bringing disciples to awakening.

"If You Meet the Buddha, Kill Him!"

One of the greatest potentialities of skillful means is to *free beings from their prisons of knowledge and prejudice*. We are often attached to our knowledge, our habits, and our prejudices, and the language of Zen must be capable of liberating us from them. According to Buddhism, knowledge is the greatest obstacle to awakening. If we are trapped by our knowledge, we will not have the possibility of going beyond it and realizing awakening. *The Sutra of One Hundred Parables* tells the story of a young widower who returned home one day to find his house burned down and his five-year-old son lost. Near the ruins of his house was the charred corpse of a child that he believed to be his son, and he wept and wept. After the child's cremation, he kept the ashes in a bag and carried them with him day and night. But his son had not actually perished in the fire. He had been taken off by bandits, and one day he escaped and returned to his father's house. The boy arrived at midnight, when his father was about to go to bed, still carrying the bag of ashes. The son knocked at the door. "Who are you?" asked the father. "I am your son." "You are lying. My son died more than three months ago." The father persisted in his belief and would not open the door. In the end the child had to leave, and the poor father lost his son forever.

When we believe something to be the absolute truth and cling to it, we cannot be open to new ideas. Even if truth itself is knocking at our door, we will not let it in. The Zen student must strive to be free of attachments to knowledge and be open so that truth may enter. The teacher must also help in these efforts. Zen master Lin Chi once said: "If you meet the Buddha, kill the Buddha. If you meet the Patriarch, kill the Patriarch." For the one who only has devotion, this declaration is terribly confusing. But its effect depends on the mentality and capacity of the one who hears. If the student is strong, she will have the capacity to liberate herself from all authority and realize ultimate reality in herself. Truth is not a concept. If we cling to our concepts, we lose reality. This is why it is necessary to "kill" our concepts so that reality can reveal itself. To kill the Buddha is the only way to see the Buddha. Any concept we have of the Buddha can impede us from seeing the Buddha in person.

"Go and Wash Your Bowl"

To return to our true home, to see into our own nature, is the aim of practice. We see into our own nature by bringing light to each act of our existence, living in a way that mindfulness is present all of the time. When walking past the cypress tree in the courtyard, we really see it. If we do not see the cypress in our own garden, how can we expect to see into our own true nature?

A Zen master who has attained awakening is someone whose eyes are open to living reality. She is someone who, after being lost in the world of concepts, has returned home to see the cypress in the courtyard and her own nature. Hence, she cannot allow her disciple to continue to wander in the world of concepts and waste his life, his own awakening. This is why the master feels compassion every time her disciple asks a question about some Buddhist principles, such as *Dharmakaya, tathata,* etc. "This young man," she thinks, "still wishes to engage in the search for reality through concepts." And she does her best to extricate the student from the world of ideas and put him in the world of living reality. Look at the cypress in the courtyard! *Look at the cypress in the courtyard!*

One day a monk asked Chao-Chou to speak to him about Zen. Chao-Chou asked, "Have you finished your breakfast?" "Yes, master, I have eaten my breakfast." "Then go and wash your bowl."

"Go and wash your bowl." This is the same as saying, "Go and live a realized life." Instead of giving the student some explanations about Zen, the master opened the door and invited the young man to enter the world of reality. "Go and wash your bowl." These words contain no secret meaning to explore or explain. They are a simple, direct, and clear declaration. There is no enigma here, nor is this a symbol. It refers to a very concrete fact.

THE GOOD REPLY

Buddhist terms, such as *tathata* (reality in itself), *svabhava* (own nature), *Dharmakaya* (the body of ultimate reality), *nirvana* (extinction), etc., suggest concepts that have nothing to do with living reality. Zen Buddhism does not consider abstractions and symbols as being important. What is important is reality itself, awakening, mindfulness. It can be understood why questions that have been asked about the tathata, Buddha, and Dharmakaya have been turned inside out by many Zen masters. Let us take the case of a question asked many times by students of Zen to their masters: "What is the Buddha?" Here are some answers that have been given:

"The Buddha? He is on the meditation hall altar."
"He is made of clay and covered with gold."
"Don't talk nonsense."
"The danger comes from your mouth."
"We are surrounded by mountains."
"Look at this man who exposes his breast and walks
     with bare feet."

These replies may embarrass us, but someone who lives in mindfulness can open the way to awakening with just such a reply. Someone who has been busy wandering in the world of abstractions can plunge directly into the heart of reality upon hearing an answer like one of these.

THE KUNG-AN AND ITS FUNCTION

There are said to be nearly 1,700 declarations or short conversations between Zen masters and their disciples that serve as *kung-an.* (Japanese: *koan,* Vietnamese: *cong-an.*) One may understand a kung-an as a kind of meditation theme, although it is not exactly a theme. The Chinese word kung-an means "official or juridical document," "a document of official value." Instead of kung-an, sometimes one uses the words *co tac (kou tso)* or *thoai dau* (*hua t'ou*), which mean, respectively, "classical formats" and "the essence of a conversation." In Zen, practitioners use kung-an as subjects for meditation until their minds come to awakening. There is a big difference between a kung-an and a math problem—the solution of the math problem is included in the problem itself, while the response to the kung-an lies in the life of the practitioner.

The kung-an is a useful instrument in the work of awakening, just as a pick is a useful instrument in working on the ground. What is accomplished from working on the ground depends on the person doing the work and not just on the pick. The kung-an is not an enigma to resolve; this is why we cannot exactly say that it is a theme or subject of meditation. A kung-an is only a skillful means to help a practitioner reach his or her goal.

Kung-an were very much in fashion during the T'ang Dynasty in China. Each Zen practitioner worked on a kung-an. Before this period, Zen masters did not use kung-an. We can therefore conclude that kung-an are not indispensable to the practice of Zen. They are skillful means created by Zen masters to help students who are working under their direction. A kung-an can also be an obstacle to awakening for a practitioner who thinks that truth is hidden in the kung-an and can be interpreted in conceptual terms.

Hakuin, a Japanese master of the Rinzai Zen sect, used to ask his disciples, "What is the sound of one hand clapping?" This is a kung-an. One reflects; one wants to know what is the sound emitted by one hand. Is there a profound significance hidden in this question? If not, why has Hakuin asked the question? If there is, how can we get at it? Like a train that always sees the rail in front of it and rushes forward, our intellect tries to establish logical principles ahead of itself while engaging in the search for truth. Suddenly, the rails are removed. Our habit-energy still tries to establish imaginary rails so that the train of the intellect can rush forward, but watch out! To continue this way is to fall into the abyss!

"What is the sound of one hand?" Such a question is the ax that cuts the rails in front of the train—it destroys the habit of conceptualization in us. If the fruit is ripe, if our spirit is well prepared, this ax-blow will be able to liberate us from the ties that have bound us for so many years to the world where we "live like a corpse" and bring us to the heart of living reality. But if we are not ready to receive it, we will continue our journey through the world of concepts. The question is right in front of us, "What is the sound of one hand?" We speculate as much as we can, we imagine this famous "sound of one hand" in a thousand different ways, and what we find we present to the master with the hope of receiving his approval. But the master always says "No!" We are at an impasse, on the point of losing our mind, and it is exactly at this point that the return to ourself begins. At that moment, "the sound of one hand" can become a sun that dazzles our whole being.

Hsiang Yen was a disciple of Master Po Chang. He was intelligent, but upon the death of his master he had still not attained awakening. He then studied under the direction of Master Wei Shan. Wei Shan asked him, "What was your face before your parents were born?" Hsiang Yen tried to answer, in vain. He retired to his room, reflected day and night, reread the texts he had studied, searched through the notes he had made during the time of Po Chang, but could not find a reply. When he presented himself to Wei Shan, the latter said to him, "I do not want to know what knowledge you have acquired; I only want to see your spiritual vision. Say something!" Hsiang Yen replied, "I do not know what to say, master. Please teach me something." But Wei Shan replied, "What use would it be if I tell you my own view?"

Hsiang Yen felt desperate. He thought his master must not want to help him, so he burned all his books and went off to a remote area saying, "Of what use is the study of Buddhist texts? I only want to live the life of a simple monk." One day, as he was preparing the ground to sow some beans, his pitch fork dislodged a pebble that struck against a bamboo stalk and went "crack." This sound brought about awakening in him. What Wei Shan had called "your face before your parents were born" suddenly dazzled in his mind. Wei Shan had refused to introduce Hsiang Yen into the world of the intellect. He wanted Hsiang Yen to return to his own true nature. The possibility of awakening came to Hsiang Yen only when he abandoned the enterprises of the intellect. The kung-an had done its work well. It had put the practitioner back on the road of spiritual experience and created a crisis that brought about real awakening.

THE SIGNIFICANCE OF THE KUNG-AN

We have discussed the function of the kung-an, but not its significance. A kung-an, to be effective, must signify *something* to the person receiving it. When a master proposes a kung-an to a student, it must be suitable to that disciple. It must be a skillful means.

The kung-an cannot be just any random word or phrase enclosing a contradiction to derail the practitioner's speculation. On the other hand, this wish to decipher a kung-an can take the practitioner into the labyrinth of philosophical reflection.

A kung-an has significance only for a specific person or group. This is the principle of skillful means. If a kung-an is used for more than one person, it is only because their mentality and psychological conditions are similar. The significance of a kung-an, therefore, exists only for those concerned and not for others.

The significance of a kung-an cannot be reduced to concepts. It is the effect produced by the kung-an itself on the mind of the one who receives it. If a kung-an is not adapted to the one for whom it is destined, it no longer has significance, even if it should come from the mouth of a great Zen master.

A monk walking through a market heard a butcher say to his customer, "This meat is of prime quality," and the mind of the monk was awakened. What the butcher said was not meant to help the monk, but *by chance*, his statement about the meat struck the already ripe mind of the monk and produced a great effect. Only the one newly enlightened saw the significance and effect of the kung-an. The butcher was entirely unaware of what had happened.

A master must know the mentality of his disciple well in order to propose a kung-an that is appropriate. Every master meets success sometimes, but also knows failure when he proposes an inappropriate kung-an.

When a former kung-an—that is to say a kung-an already proposed to another person—is recounted to us, it can sometimes happen that we reach enlightenment ourselves; all that is necessary is that the kung-an is suitable to our mind. If the kung-an does not produce an effect on us, it can be for two reasons: the first is that the kung-an is not correct for us; the second is that we are not yet ready to receive it. In either case, it is necessary to allow the kung-an to act and not to make efforts at deduction and reason in order to find in it a conceptual significance. The kung-an only has significance for the one who is in the "circle of circumstances." If we are outside this circle, it can have no meaning for us now. When we are within the circle, that is, when we find ourselves in the same condition as the one to whom the kung-an was originally addressed, it can be our kung-an. Until then, we can only plant it in the soil of our spiritual life and water it with our mindfulness. One day, it may present to us the flower of awakening.

A monk asked Chao Chou, "Does a dog have the nature of awakening?" "No," said the master. Another time, another monk asked him, "Does a dog have the nature of awakening?" Chao Chou replied, "Yes."

Why two contradictory replies to the same question? Because of the difference of the mentality of the two questioners. The answers "yes" and "no" here are skillful means aimed at producing an effect on the minds of the practitioners. Each reply does not claim to be an objective truth. On the conceptual level, objective truth is on the side of the word "yes," because in Mahayana Buddhist circles it is said that every being has the nature of awakening. But in the world of ultimate reality, the word "yes" is no longer a concept that is opposed to the concept "no." The words "yes" and "no" act here on the practitioners in different ways. That is why their "significance" can only be received subjectively by each practitioner concerned.

The "no" of Chao Chou is used by many Zen masters as a kung-an for their students. Let us listen, for example, to Master Wu Men, a Chinese monk of the thirteenth century, in his work *Wu Men Kuan*:

> To come to Zen, it is necessary to enter through the gates of the ancestors. To attain awakening, it is necessary to get to the bottom of the mind. If you

cannot pass through the gates of the ancestors, if you cannot get to the bottom of your mind, you will remain forever a ghost clinging to plants and grass. What is the gate of the ancestors? This single word "no" is the gate for the whole school of Zen. The one who can pass through this gate will be able not only to meet Chao Chou, but to walk hand-in-hand with all the other ancestors. He will see with the same eyes and hear with the same ears. What joy! Is there anyone among you who wishes to pass through this gate? If there is, I invite him to pick up the doubt mass of his body, with its 360 bones and 84,000 pores, and search for "no" day and night, without a moment's respite. Do not understand "no" as nothingness; do not take it to be a concept of nonbeing, as opposed to being. It is necessary to swallow it as you would swallow a red-hot iron ball, to rip out all the knowledge accumulated over many years. You must allow yourself to ripen slowly, and one day, you will find inner and outer to be one. You will wake up from your dream, but you will not be able to speak about it with anyone. . . . Your awakening will make the earth and sky tremble, as if you hold in your own two hands the precious sword of Kan-u. When you meet the Buddha, kill the Buddha; when you meet the ancestors, kill the ancestors. You will come to absolute freedom at the edge of the sheer cliff of life and death, and you will walk in the six realms of existence and through the

four modes of rebirth, all the while remaining in perfect concentration.[1]

How can we to reach this state? There is only one
way: mobilize the energy of your whole being and
pick up this "no" without being interrupted for a second. Then awakening will come, like the wick of a
lamp that is lit at the very moment of contact with the
flame. Listen:

The awakening nature of the dog,
   is the official decree, the concrete theme.
But if you meddle with concepts of being and
   nonbeing,
   you lose your life.

This poem of Wu Men has become a great kung-an itself.
What does Wu Men mean when he says, ". . . pick up the
doubt mass of [your] body, with its 360 bones and 84,000
pores, and search for 'no' day and night, without a moment's
respite"? It is so simple! Master Wu Men is telling us that we
must bring light to our existence. We must not allow our life
to be swallowed up by the shadows; we must not remain
plunged in forgetfulness; we must not live like a corpse. We
must be alive in each moment, in each ksana—our 360 bones

[1] The six realms are hell, hungry ghosts, beasts, fighting demons, human
beings, and devas. The four modes of rebirth are through the womb,
through eggs hatched outside the body, through moisture, and through
metamorphosis.

and 84,000 pores must be awake. In this bright light, the problem is looked at and the face of "no" revealed. This is not the play of the intellect, not just words pronounced by our lips. This is a ball of red-hot iron to swallow with your whole being. It is the problem of life and death.

Life is more than concepts. It is not necessary to get lost in our concepts. "Do not understand 'no' as nothingness; do not take it to be a concept of *nonbeing* as opposed to *being*," because "if you meddle with concepts of being and nonbeing, you lose your life." We lose our lives if we depart from living reality and dwell only in the world of conceptual phantoms. We will be a ghost, a being without flesh or bones.

ENTERING THE CIRCLE

Master Huang Po has said about the "no" of Chao Chou:

> All those who consider themselves to be knights must try this kung-an. Stay with this "no" twenty-four hours a day, whether you are sitting, standing, or lying down, and even when you are getting dressed, eating, drinking, or going to the toilet. Your mind must continually concentrate its energies on this "no." Then the flower of the mind will bloom and one day you will see the great Way of Liberation open in front

of you. After that you will no longer be deceived by
this old monk and his kung-an.

What Huang Po says does not differ from what Wu Men
said. Huang Po thoroughly endorses the importance of the
function of the kung-an as a skillful means when he speaks of
the deception of this old monk, Chao Chou, the author of the
kung-an himself.

Let us look again at the example of the cypress in the
courtyard given by Chao Chou to his disciple. The cypress in
the courtyard belongs to only two people, Chao Chou and his
disciple. One points to the cypress in the courtyard and says
to the other, "Look at the cypress in the courtyard." Imagine a
circle enclosing Chao Chou, his disciple, and the cypress. We
ourselves are outside the circle. Chao Chou points out the
cypress to his disciple, and not to us. We are only spectators,
observers. We do not really know what took place between
Chao Chou, his disciple, and the cypress. The question will
only arise for us when we have our own cypress. What does it
mean: "our own cypress"? The cypress that is in the circle will
only be ours when we enter the circle ourselves, when we
accept the kung-an as our own and are not simply studying
the kung-an of others!

A kung-an is only a kung-an when it is ours. Kung-ans of
others are not kung-ans. Thus, the cypress of the disciple of
Chao Chou is not *my* cypress. I must make the cypress *mine*.
Once it becomes mine, it is no longer his. There is no relation

between *my* cypress and *his* cypress. They are two different trees.

The first step is to reject the attitude of an observer. Grateful for Chao Chou's pointing, we can now look at the cypress with our own two eyes. Chao Chou is seated right before us, and the cypress in the courtyard is within sight. We are face-to-face with Chao Chou and with the cypress. Do you see it? If you see the cypress clearly, the kung-an is a success. Whether it is a cypress, a lemon tree, or a willow is of no importance. It can be a cloud, a river, or even this hand that I put on the table. If you see it, the kung-an is a success.

Sometimes Zen masters, instead of creating a new kung-an, use a former kung-an. This does not mean to say that they allow their disciples to play the role of observers, using only their intellects to examine the kung-ans of others. Zen masters want the former kung-ans to be renewed and the disciples to take them as their own. A monk asked Dien Ngu Giac Hoang, a Vietnamese Zen master of the thirteenth century, "What is meant by the unprecedented matter of advancement?" Referring to an ancient picture, Dien Ngu replied, "It is to carry the sun and the moon on the end of a stick." The monk replied, "What is the use of an old kung-an?" Dien Ngu smiled, "Each time it is retold, it becomes new."

If one does not see the cypress, it is because one has not been able to make the cypress into *a new cypress for oneself*—the living cypress of reality—and because one is content to go in search of the mere image of the cypress of another.

After the death of Chao Chou, a monk came to learn from one of his disciples. "Did he give any explanation about this cypress?" the monk asked. The disciple, who had reached awakening, replied, "My master never spoke about any cypress." By this time, the kung-an of the cypress was very famous. Everyone in the country was speaking about it. So why did the disciple deny a fact known by all? The monk insisted, "Everyone knows that the master himself stated the kung-an of the cypress. Why do you deny it?" The disciple of Chao Chou responded firmly, "My master *never* spoke about any cypress. Stop slandering him."

You may wonder why a disciple of Chao Chou would say this. The answer is simple: The true cypress could not be "seen." The visiting monk stayed outside the circle to "observe" the cypress, but that cypress was already dead. Chao Chou's disciple knew that it was better to "kill" the dead cypress than to affirm its existence for the monk.

The reply of Chao Chou's disciple has become a new kung-an. Looking deeply, we can see another huge cypress rise up and become revitalized. But whether you do or do not see this new cypress has nothing to do with Chao Chou's cypress.

THE MIND MUST BE RIPE

Kung-ans are not study or research material. Each kung-an must be considered a finger pointing to the reality of your own true nature as well as the reality of the world. This finger can only fulfill its role as pointer if you are *aware* that it is pointing directly at you. You must be vigilant—awake and alert—because you are face to face with the master who observes you with his penetrating look. The master can, at any moment, strike you with his stick or let out a piercing cry. It is as though you were on the edge of a precipice. It is in this state that your mind receives the jolt of the kung-an.

Here is a kung-an that shows the intense and urgent nature of the problem of "birth and death." One day Hsiang Yen said to his disciples, "A man is suspended by his teeth from a high branch, his hands and feet not holding on to anything. Another man, at the foot of the tree, asks him, 'Why did Bodhidharma come from India to China?' If our man opens his mouth to speak, he will fall and crush himself on the earth below. What must he do?" A disciple named Hu Tou presented himself and said to Hsiang Yen, "I beg you, master, do not take the case of the man clinging by his teeth. Tell us of the man who has already gotten down."

Hsiang Yen transformed an old kung-an into an entirely new one, but Hu Tou and the other students did not get the impact. Not until hundreds of years later did other students of the way realize enlightenment thanks to Hsiang Yen's kung-an.

Te Shan came to Lung T'an and stood near him right up to midnight. Then Lung T'an said to him, "It is late, why don't you go home?" Te Shan opened the door and left, but retraced his steps immediately, saying, "It is dark outside." Lung T'an then lit a candle for him but as soon as Te Shan took the candle, Lung T'an blew it out. Darkness enveloped them suddenly and awakening came to Te Shan. He bowed deeply.

Hsiang Yen, as we said earlier, once thought that Wei Shan did not want to teach him the secret of Zen. He left the monastery and retired to a distant place. But Hsiang Yen is not the only practitioner of Zen who has thought this. Many disciples ask their masters questions that they believe are important but which the latter refuse to answer. The disciples complain, "I have been here for years already, why do you treat me like a newcomer?" A monk asked master Lung T'an, "What is reality in itself (tathata)? What is supreme wisdom (prajña)?" Lung T'an replied, "I haven't the least reality in me; I do not possess supreme wisdom." Another monk interrogated Chao Chou on the essence of Zen and Chao Chou replied, "Have you had your breakfast?" When the monk replied yes, he was sent to wash his bowl. Another monk questioned Ma Tsu on the First Ancestor's intentions. Ma Tsu said, "I am very tired today, ask Te Shan." When the monk asked his older brother in the Dharma Te Shan, he said, "Why don't you ask the master?" "I have already asked our master. He said he was tired and he told me to ask you." Te Shan said, "I have a headache, ask Tche Hai." And when the monk asked his other Dharma brother Tche Hai, he replied, "I don't know."

To refuse to answer a question or to *say* something that, in appearance, has nothing to do with the question, does not mean that the teacher is refusing to help his disciple. The teacher seeks only to dislodge the disciple from the world of speculation. In fact, the teacher can always cite passages from the scriptures and give detailed explanations concerning the notions of tathata, nirvana, prajña, etc. If he does not do it, it is because he knows that such explanations will not be useful in helping bring the student to awakening.

There are also cases where explanations did help the disciples get rid of false views about a doctrine and its methods. But the master may refuse to reply or give an explanation that could hurt the chances for awakening and do harm to the disciple. Wei Shan once asked Po Chang, "Can one speak without using the throat, lips, and tongue?" Po Chang replied, "Certainly, but if I do it I destroy my whole posterity."

Lung T'an lived for years with his master, T'ien Huang, without receiving from him the secrets of Zen. One day he could keep silent no longer. "Master," he said, "I have been with you for years, but you have never transmitted anything to me. I beg you to treat me with more compassion." T'ien Huang said, "I have always transmitted to you the secrets of Zen, from the day of your entry into the monastery. When you bring me my dinner, I thank you; when you bow down in front of me, I also bow my head. Why do you say I have never transmitted to you the essence of Zen?"

Vietnamese Zen master Tinh Khong, whose disciple also reproached him for not having taught him the secret of Zen, said to this disciple, "We are living together in this temple. When you light the fire, I wash the rice. When you beg for alms, I hold the bowl for you. I have never neglected you."

To help practitioners cross the river to the shore of awakening, Zen masters hold out the staff of skillful means. But the disciple must grab hold of it. If his eyes remain shut and his mind blocked, the practitioner will miss the staff. A monk came to Vietnamese Zen master Cam Thanh, a ninth-century monk of the Vo Ngon Thong sect, and asked, "What is Buddha?" Cam Thanh said, "Everything." The monk continued, "What is the mind of Buddha?" Cam Thanh replied, "Nothing has been hidden." The monk said, "I don't understand." Cam Thanh responded, "You missed!"

Each time a staff is held out to us, we either grab it or miss it. There is no alternative. Hesitation shows that we are not yet ripe. But each time we fail, we must not regret. We can only go back to our daily work of carrying water, cooking, and cultivating the earth, striving anew with increased mindfulness.

At the time when Tri Bao, a twelfth-century Zen monk of the Vo Ngon Thong sect, had not yet reached enlightenment, another monk asked him, "Where did you come from when you were born and where will you go when you die?" Tri Bao thought about it. The monk smiled, "In the length of a thought, the clouds have crossed a thousand miles." If you are not yet ripe, all efforts at waking you up will be in vain.

Continue your daily practice of mindfulness, observing the cypress tree in your own courtyard, with all of your peace, serenity, and presence. The practice is enjoyable. There is no need to waste time or distract ourselves. Then when a real kung-an is offered to us, we will be ready.

IV

MOUNTAINS ARE
MOUNTAINS AND
RIVERS ARE RIVERS

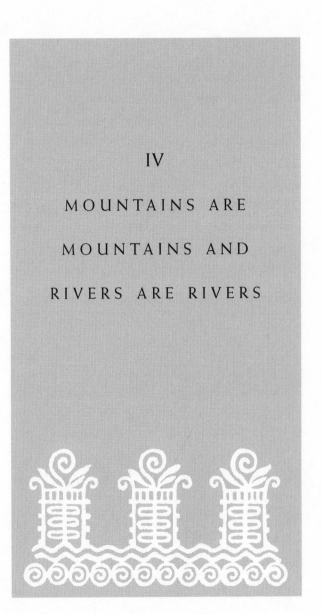

THE MIND SEAL

The authentic mind seal is *transmitted in every moment*. If the disciple deeply observes the way the master walks, eats, speaks, and performs each act of daily life, transmission can take place continuously. The ceremony of transmission is just a formality. True transmission is available to each disciple in every moment. This is real Zen, not just in books but in the living reality of relationships and daily life.

The master does not transmit his own awakening to the disciple as such. He only helps her realize the awakening already present within her. The expression to "transmit the mind seal" is essentially symbolic. The mind seal, as reality in itself (tathata), expresses the nature of awakening (*Buddhata*). According to Mahayana Buddhism, all living beings possess the nature of awakening. Therefore, the mind seal is already present in each person and does not need to be transmitted. Vinitaruci, founder of the Vietnamese Zen sect that carries his name, spoke thus to his disciple Phap Hien: "The mind seal of the Buddhas is reality itself. Nothing can be added to it, nothing can exist outside of it. One does not get it, one does not lose it. It is neither permanent nor impermanent, created nor destroyed, similar nor different. It is called a 'mind seal' only as a skillful means."

Here again one sees the methodology of Buddhism. As words and concepts, nirvana, prajña, and tathata are not really nirvana, prajña, and tathata. This is also true of the reality of awakening, which Zen calls the mind seal. It is only a concept to be used as a skillful means. It should not become an obstacle. To combat the idea that the mind seal is a thing that can be obtained, Master Vo Ngon Thon, the ninth-century founder of the Vo Ngon Thong Zen sect in Vietnam, left this message for his disciple Cam Thanh before he died:

> At the four cardinal points,
> it is said abroad
> that our founding ancestor lived in India
> and transmitted his eye of the Dharma
>   treasure called "Thien" (Zen):
> A flower, five petals,
> perpetual seeds,
> secret words, mystical symbols,
> and thousands of similar things
> are considered to belong to the mind sect of
>   immaculate nature.
> But where is India? It is right here now.
> The sun and the moon of India are the sun and the
> moon of
>   our time.

> Mountains and rivers of India are the mountains and
> rivers of
>   our time;
> To disturb something is to be attached to it,
> and to slander the Buddha and the ancestors.
> One error drags in its wake a thousand errors.
> Examine things closely,
> in order not to deceive your Dharma heirs.
> Don't question me further.
> I have nothing to say. I have said nothing.

"I have said nothing" is the conclusion of master Vo Ngon
Thong after saying a lot. One sees clearly the "letting-go"
mind of Buddhism. To say something and to say it in a way
that people do not become attached to it is the meaning of
the term "Vo Ngon Thong" (communion without words),
which is the name of this Zen master. He means that there is
no transmission to speak about and no "seal" transmitted from
generation to generation. One should not wait for awakening
from someone other than oneself, even from the master. Vo
Ngon Thong rejects the *affirmation* of the idea of transmission,
but he is also afraid that the disciples will come to the *negation*
of the idea of transmission, so he states, "One error drags in its
wake a thousand errors. . . . I have said nothing."

   To receive the mind seal is to see clearly into one's own
nature—the mind seal (or true nature) as the tathata or Buddhata is one of the great themes of the Mahayana school of

Buddhism. If Zen masters refuse questions on this subject, it is
because they want to help their disciples avoid wasting time in
speculation. In reality, "true nature," tathata and Buddhata, is
very close to the thought and practice of Zen. But the *idea* of
true nature can become an obstacle for the practitioner, even
if realization of our true nature is the very aim of Zen.

True Mind and False Mind

Huang Po, in speaking of the reality of true nature (what he
called "the mind of unity and thusness"), said:

> Buddhas and living beings participate in the same
> pure and unique mind. There is no separation con-
> cerning this mind. Since time immemorial this mind
> has never been created or destroyed; it is neither
> green nor yellow; it has neither form nor aspect; it is
> neither being nor nonbeing; it is neither old nor new,
> neither short nor long, neither big nor small. It tran-
> scends all intellectual categories, all words and expres-
> sions, all signs and marks, all comparisons and dis-
> criminations. It is what it is; if one tries to conceive it,
> one loses it. Unlimited like space, it has no boundaries
> and cannot be measured. This mind is unity and thus-
> ness. It is Buddha.

This statement of Huang Po is clear. We must allow the mind to reveal itself. It is lost the moment we try to conceptualize it. This means that in order to realize it, we must take a road other than that of concepts. The only way to realize this mind of unity and thusness, which is also called true mind, is to return to ourselves and see into our true nature.

True mind is the radiant nature of being, while false mind is the faculty of conceiving and discriminating. When we realize true mind, living reality is revealed in its completeness; it is the enlightened life of Zen. The world built of concepts is different from living reality. The world in which birth and death, good and bad, and being and nonbeing are opposed exists only for those who do not live an awakened life. The vicissitudes of life no longer dominate the consciousness of an "awakened" person because she has already entered the world of reality and does not discriminate between birth and death, good and bad, being and nonbeing.

In *The Awakening of Faith in the Mahayana (Mahayana Sraddhotpada)*, we read:

> All phenomena of being, since time immemorial, are independent of concepts and words. Concepts and words cannot transform them or separate them from their true nature.

This Mahayanist work uses the expression *"wu-nien,"* "nonconceptual." Non-conceptual understanding is not based on

the concepts of the false mind. It is also called non-discriminative understanding (nirvikalpajñana).

REALITY IN ITSELF

True nature, or true mind, is not what we would call an idealis-
tic, ontological entity. It is reality itself. The word "mind" is
sometimes called "nature." True mind and true nature are
names for the same reality. From the standpoint of knowledge,
we call it "understanding," or sometimes "mind." When we are
talking about reality in itself, the distinction between the subject and the object of knowledge dissolves, so we use expressions like "true nature," "true mind," "non-discriminative understanding," or *seeing into one's own nature.*

Zen thought is the crystallization of the thought of all
Mahayana Buddhist schools. Its notion of *tathagata dhyana* is
derived from the *Lankavatara.* The Zen notion of true mind,
radiant and miraculous, comes from the *Suramgama.* Its notion
of the merits of *dhyana* comes from the *Mahavaipulyapurnabuddha.* Its notion of interbeing comes from *Avatamsaka.* Its notion
of emptiness is derived from the *Prajñaparamita.* The synthesis
of all these currents of Buddhist thought is accomplished in
Zen quite naturally, just as plants absorb air, water, and light.

True mind is not born at the moment of awakening, because it is neither created nor destroyed. Awakening only reveals it. This is also true of nirvana and Buddhata. The *Mahaparinirvana Sutra* says:

> The substance and the cause of nirvana is the nature of awakening—Buddhata. The Buddhata does not produce nirvana. This is why we say nirvana-without-cause, or uncreated. . . . The nature of awakening among living beings is the same. Although living beings appear and are transformed, they always dwell in the nature of awakening.

Consequently, the practitioner need not wait for some awakening to come from outside, some transmission or gift of wisdom. Wisdom cannot be obtained. The mind cannot transmit itself. The *Heart Sutra* (*Mahaprajñaparamita Hridya Sutra*) assures us that there is no obtaining because there is no object to obtain. Twelfth-century Vietnamese Zen master Nguyen Hoc told his disciples: "Do not wait for another person to transmit awakening."

All that is created and destroyed, all that can be obtained and lost, is conditioned. A thing is produced when the conditions necessary to its production come together. A thing is lost when conditions are no longer favorable. Reality in itself is the base of everything. It is not conditioned by production or destruction, by gain or loss. Master Nguyen Hoc says, "True nature is non-nature. It has nothing to do with production or destruction." However, to say that it exists in a world in itself independent of the world of phenomena would be to commit the gravest of errors regarding the problem of true mind. To say, for example, "A world exists which is real in itself" already classifies this world in the category of *being*, in opposition to the category of *nonbeing*. Both being or nonbeing, as we have said, belongs to the conceptual world. If the world of true mind transcends the world of concepts, why classify it using concepts? It would cease to be the world of true mind. It would become just a concept—vaguer and more impoverished even than other concepts. Words cannot describe true mind, concepts cannot express true mind. The way to speak of true mind is through skillful means, as Vinitaruci says. To say a thing is easy but most people will allow themselves to be taken in by the thing said, so it is better to say nothing, to "understand without words."

As for the world of phenomena, we are inclined to believe that it is illusory, separate from reality. And we think that only by ridding ourselves of it will we be able to reach the world of true mind. That is also an error. This world of birth and death, this world of lemon trees and maple trees, *is the world of reality in itself.* There is no reality that exists outside of the lemon and maple trees. The sea is either calm or stormy. If you want a calm sea, you cannot get it by suppressing the stormy sea. You must wait for the same sea to become calm. The world of reality is that of lemon and maple trees, of mountains and rivers. If you *see* it, it is present in its complete reality. If you do not, it is a world of ghosts and concepts, of birth and death.

THE LAMP AND LAMPSHADE

The Ts'ao T'ung Zen sect (Soto Zen in Japan), applies these five principles to meditation:

1. Sitting meditation, even without a subject of meditation, is enough.
2. Sitting meditation and awakening are not two different things.
3. One must not wait for awakening.
4. There is no awakening to attain.
5. Mind and body are one.

These principles do not contradict the method based on the use of the kung-an in the Lin Chi sect (Rinzai in Japan). In fact, the Ts'ao T'ung principles can help the practitioners of the Lin Chi sect not discriminate between ends and means. Many practitioners are inclined to think that sitting medita-tion is a means to attain awakening. But when we turn from forgetfulness to mindfulness, this state is already true awaken-ing. This is why the Ts'ao T'ung sect has said, "To practice sitting meditation is already to be a Buddha." When we truly sit, we are already fully awakened.

In our usual state of forgetfulness, we lose ourselves and we lose our life. To practice sitting meditation is to recover ourselves. Visualize the different parts of your mind and body dispersed throughout space. To practice sitting meditation is to bring them back together, to regain the unity and whole-ness of our being, to bring ourselves to life, to become a Buddha.

Sitting meditation is a great joy. The lotus or half lotus position makes it easier to breathe freely, to concentrate deeply, and to return to the state of mindfulness. But Zen should not be practiced only in the sitting position. We can practice as well while walking, eating, talking, working, and in all positions and activities. "What is a Buddha?" "A Buddha is one who lives twenty-four hours a day in mindfulness."

A monk asked Hsiang Lin, "Why did the First Ancestor come to China?" Hsiang Lin replied, "It ruins the health to sit for too long." This same question has been given a variety of replies by many masters. Master Kieu Feng replied, "The fur of a tortoise weighs twenty pounds." Master Tsong Chan said, "Wait until the River Tong changes direction and I will tell you." These replies produce particular effects in particular minds. But the reply given by Hsiang Lin, "It ruins your health to sit for too long" is simple and can be applied to everyone. To sit with only the intention of finding the meaning of a kung-an is not real Zen meditation; it is a waste of one's time and one's life. To practice sitting meditation is not just to reflect on a kung-an, but to light the lamp of awareness in ourselves. If we do that, the meaning of the kung-an will reveal itself quite naturally. But if the lamp of awareness is not lit in us, we will continue to sit in the shadows of life and will never see into our own nature. That is why the master said we will ruin our health if we sit for too long!

The kung-an is not a subject of research; sitting meditation is not a research project. Sitting meditation is life, and the kung-an helps us test, witness, and maintain vigilance in our life. It is sometimes said that the kung-an is the lampshade, and Zen is the lamp itself.

A Non-Conceptual Experience

Sitting meditation is not to think, reflect, or lose ourselves in concepts or discriminations. It is also not to remain immobile, like a stone or the trunk of a tree. How can we avoid two extremes of conceptualization and inertia? By dwelling the present moment, right in the midst of our experience, under the lamp of mindfulness. Direct experience and awareness of direct experience are the ways to avoid these extremes. These words may seem complicated, but the experience itself is quite straightforward.

When you have some tea, for example, you have a direct experience of the tea. This experience can be enjoyed in full mindfulness. The experience of drinking tea is not a concept.

It is only later, when you reflect on it and distinguish between this and other experiences, that drinking tea becomes a concept. Our concept of drinking tea is not this experience itself; so, strictly speaking, we cannot say that our experience has *become* a concept.

At the moment of the experience, you and the taste of tea are one. There is no differentiation. The tea is you, and you are the tea. There is not the drinker of tea and the tea being enjoyed, because there is no distinction between subject and object in the real experience. When we start to distinguish subject and object, the experience disappears, and only our concepts remain. *The world of Zen is the world of pure experience without concepts.* To introduce a kung-an as a subject of meditation is not, in itself, to practice Zen. This is the reason why the Ts'ao T'ung sect says, "Sitting meditation, even without a subject of meditation, is enough."

The world of direct experience of Zen is, therefore, that of life and of awareness, and not of inert matter. On a conceptual level, if we can make the distinction between the one who tastes the tea and the tea that is tasted, which are two elements basic to the experience of the tea (a single experience without subject or object), we can also make the distinction between the practitioner of Zen and the reality lived by him in his experience. This spiritual experience is produced when the practitioner and his reality (the psycho-physiological stream of his own existence) enter into direct communion. The nature of this experience, like that of the tea, is also indivisible. But we must remember that even the notion of "unity" is just another concept. Life is not a representation of life. Reality in itself transcends all descriptions and ideas. The world of Zen is the world of tathata itself.

THE PRINCIPLE OF NON-DUALITY

Japanese Zen master Dogen said, "All phenomena are mind; mind is all. Mind contains rivers, mountains, moon, and sun." In Zen experience there is no longer an object of knowledge. Nagarjuna's *Treatise of Great Understanding* (*Mahaprajñaparamita Sastra*) says:

> All phenomena can be understood to be in two categories: mind and matter. On the conceptual level, we distinguish mind and matter, but on the level of awakening, all is mind. Object and mind are both marvelous. Mind is matter, matter is mind. Matter does not exist outside of mind. Mind does not exist outside of matter. Each is in the other. This is called the "nonduality of mind and matter."

When we discriminate between subject and object, we are removed from Zen and its guiding principle of nonduality. Look at Figure One below. Reality is represented as a circle divided into two parts A, mind, and B, matter.

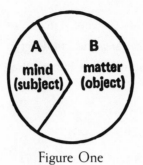

Figure One

It seems possible for us to distinguish between mind and
matter, subject and object. But to do so is, in reality, artificial
if not impossible. First of all, mind, generally considered to be
the subject of knowledge, can also be the object of knowledge. And when mind becomes its own object of knowledge,
is that which is apprehended mind itself or just a projection of
mind? Are psychological phenomena, considered as objects of
study and analysis, our mind itself or only images and concepts that we use to represent the mind? Can the mind enter
into itself, or is it only capable of seeing its image, of moving
around on the periphery of itself? Another question: does
mind exist independently of its object? Or to put it another
way: can the subject of knowledge exist without the existence
of its object?

The doctrine of Vijñanavada, one of the Mahayana Buddhist schools, says that the word "knowledge" (*vijñana*) indicates *at the same time* the subject and the object of knowledge.
The subject and object of knowledge cannot exist independently of each other. A does not exist if B does not exist, and
vice versa.

For reasons already given, the division of reality into mind and matter, subject and object, must be considered as superficial and conventional, and also as skillful means. When reality is revealed in the light of mindfulness, mind is revealed as true mind, and matter as true matter. The *Treatise of Great Understanding* says, "Mind is matter. Matter is mind. Matter does not exist outside of mind. Mind does not exist outside of matter."

Consider Figure Two:

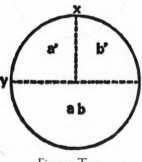

Figure Two

Reality (ab) is symbolized by the circle. This is the Dharmakaya, the tathata, nirvana (the *perfection*, the *totality*, the *unconditioned*), which transcend all mental categories and all concepts. Above the dotted line (y), two parts are distinguished which themselves are separated by the dotted line (x), distinguishing the subject of knowledge (a') and the object of knowledge (b').

The knowledge of a' b' is in this case conceptual knowledge. It is based on the dualistic notion of reality, existence separated into mind and matter. This form of knowledge has vikalpa as its nature, that is to say, *discrimination-imagination*, and cannot introduce us directly into reality.

Let us now look at Figure Three:

Figure Three

Here the two dotted lines (y and x) have been removed. The subject (a′) and the object (b′) return to themselves, in perfect, non-discriminative and non-imaginative reality. This is the world of awakening of Zen.

Now let us look at Figure Four:

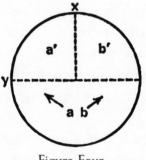

Figure Four

In this figure we see the two dotted lines (y and x) reappear. Arising from non-discriminative and non-imaginative reality, (a b) is expressed in the subject (a') and in the object (b'). Figure Four is similar to Figure Two, but in this case there are, in addition, two small arrows that indicate the movement of remanifestation.

An awakened person lives in the material world the same as everyone else. When she sees a rose, she knows that it is a rose, like everyone else. But she is neither conditioned nor imprisoned by concepts. Concepts now become marvelous skillful means in her possession. An awakened person looks, listens, and distinguishes things, all the while being perfectly aware of the presence (a b) that is the perfect and non-discriminative nature of everything. She sees deeply the nature of interbeing.

INTERBEING

The "interbeing" nature of things corresponds directly with the concept of not-self discussed earlier. To see things in their interbeing nature is to perceive their nature of interdependence, not having a separate, independent self. Look, for example, at a table. We recognize its existence only when the conditions upon which its presence depends converge. We cannot recognize its existence before these conditions come together. Before being there, the table existed in the wood, the saw, the nails, the carpenter, and the many other elements directly and indirectly connected. When we can see the existence of the table through these interdependent elements, we can also see it in unlimited space and infinite time. This vision of reality delivers us from the fears that result from such concepts as non-existence, impermanence, and not-self. Awakened, we are free, serene, and happy, masters of ourselves. Figure Four represents the state of awakening, while Figure Two represents the state of sleep, even though the two figures are virtually identical. A Zen master said, "Before practicing Zen, rivers were rivers and mountains were mountains. When I practiced Zen, I saw that rivers were no longer rivers and mountains no longer mountains. Now I see that rivers are again rivers and mountains are again mountains." Figures Two, Three, and Four support this testimony. Once awakening is reached, we are masters of ourselves, even while living in the world of conditioned things. Concerning the relation between matter and mind, phenomena and true nature, knowledge and action, Cuu Chi, an eleventh-century Vietnamese monk of the Vo Ngon Thong sect, said:

All methods aiming at the realization of awakening have their origin in your true nature. The true nature of everything is in your mind. Mind and matter are one, not two different things. Conditioning, servitude, and error do not truly exist. True and false, merit and sin, are illusory images. So is the law of cause and effect. As long as your activity is based on conceptual discrimination, it is not free. The free person sees all, because he knows that there is nothing to be seen. He perceives all, not being deceived by concepts. When he looks at things, he sees their true nature. When he perceives things, he penetrates their nature of interbeing. Thus, while living in the world he possesses the secret of the arising and manifestation of phenomena. This is the only way to arrive at awakening. Free of errors caused by concepts, he lives in peace and freedom, even in the world of karma. Using skillful means, he realizes his calling of awakening in this conditioned world, without thinking whether the world is conditioned or unconditioned.

V

FOOTPRINTS OF

EMPTINESS

THE BIRTH OF ZEN BUDDHISM

Toward the end of the eighth century, the term "Zen school" was used for the first time. Before this the terms *Leng Chia Tsung, Tung Ch'an Tsung, Ta Ma Tsung, Ho So Tsung, Nieu T'ou Tsung*, etc., were used—all these terms representing Buddhist traditions that considered sitting meditation to be the core practice and basis of Buddhism.

In the middle of the fifth century, the Indian monk Gunabhadra (394–468) translated the *Lankavatara Sutra* into Chinese. His disciples and their friends organized study sessions of the text and formed a school called *Leng Chia Tsung* (Lankavatara school). The *Lankavatara* is generally considered a basic text for Zen Buddhism.

In the seventh century, a Chinese monk named Tao Shin founded a monastery dedicated to the practice of meditation on Mount Tung Shan at Ho Nan. One of his disciples, Hung Jen, continued his work and taught the practice of Zen to certain disciples, including such celebrated monks as Shen Hsiu, Hui Neng, and Fa Jung. Shen Hsiu later taught in the north of the country and Hui Neng in the south. Fa Jung (594–647) remained at the monastery Yeo Ts'i on the mountain of Niu T'ou at Nan King. Zen started to break up with the

Tsing T'ou (*Amidaism*). According to most authorities, Fa Jung
(594–647) is considered to be the founder of the Niu T'ou
sect, but in fact he was neither the disciple of Tao Shin nor the
founder of the sect in question. The tradition founded by Tao
Shin and Hung Jen is called the Tung Shan sect. Both taught
in the monastery on Tung Shan mountain.

Shen Hsiu founded the Northern school (Pei Tsung). It
was in this school that the use of the kung-an was started. Hui
Neng founded the Southern school (Nan Tsung), but in effect
it was his disciple Shen Hui (668–760) who was the true
founder. Most of the historical documents of Chinese Zen
Buddhism arise from this school. It is also the Southern school
that developed the notion of *sudden enlightenment*, while the
Northern school embraced the doctrine of *gradual enlightenment*.

To assure the grandeur and prestige of the Southern
school, Shen Hui felt it necessary to establish a history of the
tradition of Zen Buddhism. Using available facts, he retraced
the lineage of Indian Buddhism, with its twenty-eight ancestors, from the Buddha and Mahakasyapa to Bodhidharma, the
First Ancestor of the Zen school in China. After him the mind
seal was transmitted to Hui Ko, then to Seng Ts'ang, Tao Shin,
Hung Jen, and Hui Neng. According to Shen Hui, Hui Neng
is the Sixth Ancestor of the Zen school. Shen Hui himself is
considered the legitimate successor of Hui Neng.

The historical documents of Zen furnished by the Southern school aimed at consolidating the prestige of this school,
and therefore do not reflect the entire truth, especially concerning the Northern school. Shen Hui attacked the Northern

school, while the latter was in vogue, because the idea of gradual enlightenment preached by this school was taken up enthusiastically by the aristocracy and the courtiers. At this time, the expression "Zen school" was not yet used, but rather the traditional appellation "Bodhidharma school" (Ta Ma Tsung).

At the same time in Niu T'ou, the monk Huian Sou (668–752) was exploring the doctrine of *no words or letters*. This doctrine, as well as the use of the kung-an started by the Northern school, was to affect the development of all the Zen sects in future generations.

When the Northern school started to decline, the Southern school experienced a rapid development. After Shen Hui, great monks like Hsi Ch'ien (700–790), Tao Yi (707–786), and Fa Kin (714–792) appeared, and the five famous schools of Zen—Lin Chi, Ts'ao T'ung, Yun Men, Kuei Yang, and Fa Yen —were founded. These schools were later introduced in Japan and Vietnam, particularly the Lin Chi and Ts'ao T'ung schools.

After Shen Hui, the tradition was called the Ho Tso school, after the place Shen Hui lived. The expression "Zen school" (*Ch'an Tsung*) appeared at the time of Po Chang (720–814), the author of the famous Zen monastic rules. Called Po Chang Ts'ing Kuei, these were the rules by which the Zen tradition separated itself completely from the monasteries of the Vinaya school.

Zen derives from a form of Buddhism that arose in a geographic zone influenced by Chinese culture. The Chinese Zen tree, transplanted in Japan, Vietnam, and Korea, has grown well and flourished. Zen Buddhism, in each of these countries, differs with certain nuances from that practiced in China, but one can easily recognize its identity.

ZEN AND THE WEST

Many scholars, monks, artists, popularizers, and lay practitioners have worked to transplant Zen to Europe and America. Have these efforts proved successful?

From the standpoint of knowledge, scholars, including Suzuki, Edward Conze, Richard Robinson, and Robert Thurman, have contributed a great deal toward arousing the interest of Westerners in Zen Buddhism. Zen has influenced the thinking of theologians like Paul Tillich, and philosophers like Erich Fromm and Carl Jung. Does Zen exist yet in the West as a living tradition? Many monks, nuns, and lay teachers are offering the practice of Zen there, but to me, much of the practice remains Oriental, foreign to Western culture. The process of Zen finding roots in Western soil is an ongoing one. Cultural, economic, and psychological conditions are different in the West. One cannot become a practitioner of Zen just by imitating the way of eating, sitting, or dressing of Chinese or Japanese practitioners. *Zen is life; Zen does not imitate.* If Zen is to fully take root in the West, it must acquire a Western form, different from Oriental Zen.

ZEN AND CHINA

There are important differences between the Indian mentality and the Chinese mentality that gave birth in China to the form of Buddhism called Zen. The Chinese are very practical people. Confucianism, Taoism, and Buddhism reflect this. The declaration made by Bodhidharma on his arrival in China has become the foundation of the Zen Buddhist tradition, because this declaration corresponds so well to the pragmatic nature of the Chinese. The Indian world of ideas and images, such as those revealed in the *Avatamsaka, Saddharma Pundarika, Vimalakirtinirdesa,* and other sutras, have no equivalent in China. Perhaps this tendency toward dreaming and speculation was one of the causes of the decline of Indian Buddhism at the beginning of the eighth century. Buddhism, which is founded on human experience and not on speculation, cannot exist without returning to concrete spiritual experience as its base. The Chinese did study and understand the fantastic world of ideas and images of Indian Mahayana Buddhism. In fact, they translated, commented upon, and systematized all the literary sources of Indian Buddhism. But their practical nature attracted them particularly to the experiential base of Buddhism, and it was this that permitted Buddhism to become firmly established on Chinese soil. Though Zen is a Chinese form of Buddhism, it reflects entirely the spirit and splendor of Indian Buddhism, from its inception to its full development. For this reason we can say that Zen brings to us the authentic spirit of Buddhism.

The experiential and pragmatic nature of Zen, its attitude vis-à-vis words and concepts, are witness to this authenticity. The Buddha in the Avatamsaka, Shingon, and T'ien T'ai sects is represented allegorically. *In Zen, the Buddha is represented as a human being of flesh and bones.* Master Lin Chi said,

> If the Buddha is immortal, why did he have to die between two sala trees in the forest of Kusinagara? Where is he now? The Buddha, just like us, must obey the law of birth and death. You say that Buddha possesses miraculous powers. But the Asuras and Brahma possess these miraculous powers too. Are they Buddhas? The miraculous powers of Buddha allow him to be free of forms when he enters the world of form, free of sounds when he enters the world of sound, free of smells when he enters the world of smell, free of tastes when he enters the world of taste, free of perceptions when he enters the world of perception, free of thoughts when he enters the world of thought. To acquire the six miraculous powers is to understand the nature of emptiness of the six sense fields. Although he is there, in his body of five aggregates, he walks on the earth using these miraculous powers.

Although different from Indian Buddhism in form and practice, in the end Zen seems to be more authentic than many other Buddhist schools. In particular, Zen emphasizes the necessity of practice leading toward enlightenment, which is the very foundation of Buddhism.

As we know, the principle of not-self is used only as a means to open the way of Buddhism—it is not a dogma. The principle of not-self is applied to both the world of living beings and the world of inanimate things. Not-self signifies absence of permanent identity. Not-self is impermanence itself. Everything is constantly changing. Therefore, nothing can be fixed in its identity. Everything is subject to not-self.

THE NOTION OF EMPTINESS

The notion of *emptiness* (*sunyata*) in Buddhism is derived from the notion of not-self. We must always ask, "Empty of what?" Emptiness, here, means empty of a separate, independent entity called a self. But empty of a separate self means full of everything!

Let us look at this passage from the *Samyutta Nikaya*:

- ⬥ Lord, why is the world called empty?
- ⬥ It is because in the world a separate self and things possessing a separate self do not exist.
- ⬥ What are the things that do not have a separate self?
- ⬥ Eye, form, and sight do not possess a separate self,

nor that which belongs to a separate self. In the
same way, ear, nose, tongue, body, thoughts, their
object, and their knowledge do not possess a separate self either, nor that which belongs to a separate
self.

All phenomena (physical, psychological, and physiological) are devoid of a permanent identity. To be empty is not to
be non-existent. It is to be without a permanent identity. To
illustrate this point, Nagarjuna, in his *Mahaprajñaparamita Sastra*
(second century) said: "It is due to emptiness that all phenomena exist." There is nothing ambiguous in this declaration. If
things are considered in the light of impermanence and not-
self, it is impossible that they should be permanent or with an
absolute identity. Existence would be impossible if things were
not empty of an absolute self. If they were not impermanent,
how could a grain of corn grow into an ear of corn? How
could your little girl grow up into a beautiful young lady?
How could totalitarian regimes ever come to an end? To affirm
that there is an absolute identity is to deny the existence of
things, while the proclamation of the principle of not-self is an
affirmation of life. Things are possible only when they are
devoid of a fixed identity. This can be expressed in these
formulas:

| Impermanence | = | not-self | = | things exist. |
| Permanence | = | fixed identity | = | nothing can exist. |

The notion of *emptiness*, according to Buddhism, is therefore the affirmation of the existence of things and not their negation. Our desire for a world in which things are permanent and indestructible is neither realizable nor desirable.

COMPLEMENTARY NOTIONS

The early schools of Buddhism (such as the Sarvastivada, Sautrantika, and Theravada) have, for this reason, established philosophical systems that aim at demonstrating that things with permanent identities do not exist, while things (dharmas) that are devoid of absolute identity do exist.

However, to avoid confusion between identity and existence, these schools teach that things exist *only in the present moment.* These schools, particularly the Sarvastivada, study and analyze physical, physiological, and psychological phenomena and also phenomena that cannot be classified in these three categories. Works devoted to these studies and analyses are numerous. The fear of nothingness, brought about by misunderstandings of the doctrine of not-self, gave rise to the need to confirm the existence of things. But in proclaiming that things exist only in the present moment, some difficulties have been created. How can we explain karma, rebirth, and enlightenment, for example, if we cannot establish the relation between things that exist in the present moment and things that existed in the past or will exist in the future?

The early Buddhist schools developed other ideas to complete their doctrine. In the Sarvastivada school, for example, it is taught that from the standpoint of the noumena, things exist in the past, present, and future, but from the standpoint of phenomena, they exist only in the present moment. The formula "identity does not exist, things exist" is not completed by the formula "the true nature of things exists in a continuous way through the past, present, and future."

The Theravada school uses the notion of obtainment to establish the relation of cause and effect between things. The Sautrantika school uses the notion of seeds (*bijas*), perfumation or habit-energy (*vasana*), and lineage (*gotra*). The Sarvastivada school teaches a pluralist-realist doctrine, a sort of pan-realism, and devotes its time to the study and analysis of ideas about dharmas.

ANTI-SCHOLASTIC REACTIONS

Reacting against these scholastic and dogmatic tendencies, new schools and doctrines arose. In the middle of the fourth century B.C.E., the Mahasanghika school again posed the problem of knowledge. It emphasized the importance of purifying the mind in order to realize enlightenment. Showing the futility of study and analysis of dharmas, this school encouraged direct spiritual experience.

The Pudgalavada school, originating at the beginning of

the third century B.C.E., proclaimed that the self exists and that the point of view of the Sthavira schools concerning the notion of not-self is contrary to the spirit of Buddhism. Although condemned as heretical by many, the Pudgalavada were able to demonstrate many errors committed within the scholastic and dogmatic tendencies of tradition. Of the 250,000 Buddhist monks in India at that time, nearly one fourth were Pudgalavadin monks.

The second century B.C. saw the appearance of the first *Prajñaparamita Sutra* text and the rise of the doctrine of *emptiness*, in an effort aimed at regaining the original spirit of Buddhism. The *Prajñaparamita* texts, as well as other Mahayana texts, such as the *Sadharmapundarika, Lankavatara, Mahaparinirvana,* and *Avatamsaka,* continued to appear in the following century. The explorations made by the Mahasanghika schools and by the Pudgalavada contributed much to the appearance of these Mahayana schools.

To see the characteristics of Zen better, we must examine the essential traits of the Sunyatavada school and the Vijñanavada school. The Sunyatavada school, known later as Madhyamika, is founded on the *Prajñaparamita* scriptures, while the Vijñanavada school is based on the *Sandhinirmocana, Lankavatara,* and other texts. These texts are all used in the Zen tradition. To me, Zen Buddhism reflects the essence of all these Mahayana scriptures in a most harmonious way.

The point of departure of *Prajñaparamita* thought is the notion of *emptiness*. In the beginning, as we know, the word *emptiness* signified the absence of a permanent self. When the Sarvastivada school declared that from the phenomenal point of view, things do not exist as permanent identities, but that the true nature of things exists from the ontological standpoint, it can be seen that this permanent identity of things became disguised as an ontological entity. The *Prajñaparamita* explains: "Things do not have their own nature; the ontological entity of things does not exist." The *Prajñaparamita*, through this declaration, brings us back to the source of Buddhism.

The notions of impermanence, not-self, interbeing, and emptiness are means aimed at revealing the errors of knowledge rather than at giving a description of the objects of knowledge. These notions must be considered as *methods* and not as *information*. According to the *Vajracchedika Prajñaparamita*, this is the most important problem of all. The Buddha said to Subhuti, who asked him what was the method to attain correct understanding:

> This is how the bodhisattva mahasattvas master their thinking. "However many species of living beings there are—whether born from eggs, from the womb, from moisture, or spontaneously; whether they

have form or do not have form; whether they have perceptions or do not have perceptions; or whether it cannot be said of them that they have perceptions or that they do not have perceptions, we must lead all these beings to the ultimate nirvana so that they can be liberated. And when this innumerable, immeasurable, infinite number of beings has become liberated, we do not, in truth, think that a single being has been liberated."

Why is this so? If, Subhuti, a bodhisattva holds on to the idea that a self, a person, a living being, or a life span exists, that person is not an authentic bodhisattva.

Why are ideas the source of errors that must be corrected? Because the idea is not reality. "To lead all beings to nirvana" is reality itself; but "to lead," "all beings," "nirvana," "the bringer," and the "brought" are only concepts. And why is there such a great distance between reality and the concept? In reality in itself, there is no discrimination. But in the world of concepts "reality" is full of discriminations: subject/object, self/not-self, etc. This is not truly reality but an erroneous image of reality. The origin of this erroneous image is called *discrimination* or *imagination* (vikalpa) in the Vijñanavadin school.

The flower that is near the window is a true flower in its undiscriminated reality. As soon as we discriminate, it is no longer revealed. In its place stands an erroneous image. The

word "empty," which at first signified the absence of permanent identity, now acquires another meaning: the image created by the concept does not represent any reality, it is imaginary.

THE A WHICH IS NOT A IS TRULY A

In the *Vajracchedika-prajñaparamita*, we find many expressions
given in the form, "The A which is not A is truly A." Let us
take these examples: "What the Tathagata calls a living being is not in essence a living being. That is why it is called
a living being." "Subhuti, what is called a conception of
dharmas is not a conception of dharmas. That is why it is
called a conception of dharmas." This means that *reality is
only reality when it is not grasped conceptually.* What we construct through our concepts is not reality. "This flower,
which is not a concept, is truly a flower." Here again is the
rejection of the principle of a permanent self and of the
tendency to see things by means of the go-between of conceptualization. The practitioner of the Way must enter into
direct contact with reality without allowing concepts to separate him from this reality. Reality cannot be conceived, nor
can it be described in words. *Reality is reality; it is thus.* This
is the significance of the word *thusness* (tathata).

The *Prajñaparamita* begins with this declaration: there is *no*
true nature, there is *no* permanent self. *Emptiness* was offered as

a means. When we begin to take it as the reality, we need an antidote.

The *Maharatnakuta* says:

Attachment to erroneous views is comparable to a sickness. All erroneous views can be cured, only attachment to the view of emptiness is incurable. Attachments to the view of being piled as high as a great mountain are preferable to attachment to nonbeing.[1]

For this reason true emptiness is identical to the tathata, which is non-discriminated and non-conceptualized reality. Many go too far in seeing emptiness or tathata as the ontological basis of everything. The idea of an ontological entity, as we already know, is the notion of an absolute self in disguise, which is the enemy of the *Prajñaparamita*. All that can be said is that emptiness or tathata is non-conceptualized reality. All concepts about emptiness are the enemies of emptiness, all concepts about the tathata are the enemies of the tathata. To arrive at the reality of emptiness or tathata will be to arrive at the Great Understanding. Let us read this dialogue in the *Astasahasrika Prajñaparamita*:

Subhuti: It is truly marvelous that the tathata can reveal the true nature of things when nothing can be said about this true nature of things! Have I understood

[1] *Kasyapa parivarta* of the *Maharatnakuta Sutra*.

you correctly, Lord, when I say that we cannot say anything about things themselves?

Buddha: It is true; we cannot speak about things.

Subhuti: And things that transcend words, can they grow or diminish?

Buddha: No, they cannot.

Subhuti: If it is thus, the six practices of the paramita[2] cannot progress. How then can the bodhisattva arrive at complete enlightenment? How can we realize complete enlightenment without perfecting the six paramitas?

Buddha: Subhuti, nothing grows or diminishes in the nature of the six paramitas. The bodhisattva who practices the paramita of generosity, who develops the paramita of generosity, and who practices skillful means never thinks, "This paramita of generosity is in the process of growing or declining." On the contrary, he thinks "The paramita of generosity is nothing other than words." When the bodhisattva offers something to someone he offers his whole heart and all the merits of this act as a gift of wisdom to all beings. This offering expresses the method of realization of total generosity. When he

[2] The six practices that lead to absolute enlightenment are generosity, discipline, patience, diligence, meditation, and wisdom.

practices discipline, patience, diligence, meditation, and wisdom he acts in the same way.

Subhuti: And what is complete enlightenment?

Buddha: It is tathata. Tathata neither increases nor decreases. If the mind of the bodhisattva remains at peace in the tathata, the bodhisattva is close to complete enlightenment; and he can never lose this. Reality transcends words and concepts and does not contain the paramitas, or dharmas, neither does it increase or decrease. When the bodhisattva remains in this mind, he is one close to complete enlightenment.

PENETRATING TATHATA

The identification of tathata with emptiness is an attempt to prevent people from conceptualizing emptiness. Similarly, the *Mahaprajñaparamita Sastra* puts forward the expression *non-empty* (*asunyata*). The *non-empty* is another name for *emptiness* and for *tathata*. The non-empty is treated in the *Mahayana Sraddhotpada* by Asvaghosa in a very appropriate way. After confirming that the tathata of things cannot be described by words or represented by concepts, Asvaghosa states that a method exists by which to penetrate tathata; it consists of "following skillfully." According to Asvaghosa, this supposes abandoning our dual-

abandoning our dualistic tendencies. When we speak of something, we do not distinguish the subject who speaks from the
object spoken of. When we see something, we do not distinguish the subject who sees from the object seen. When we are
able to transcend discrimination, we begin to penetrate the
world of tathata. "Following skillfully," according to Asvaghosa, is to clear a path amid the words and concepts in
order to arrive at reality.

Words and concepts can be used without allowing ourselves to be taken in by them. In fact, words and concepts can
be quite useful and even indispensable. On the level of words
and concepts, two forms of tathata can be distinguished—
emptiness and non-emptiness. It is because emptiness is not a
concept that one calls it *true emptiness*, and it is because non-
emptiness is not a concept either that one calls it *true non-
emptiness*. All of this is designed to combat the *concept of emptiness*,
which is the primary enemy of emptiness.

SUBJECT AND OBJECT

Discrimination between subject and object (a dualistic tendency) is the cause of all error concerning both knowledge
and practice. The attitude of the *Prajñaparamita* vis-à-vis
knowledge and method is expressed very clearly in this passage from the *Astasahasrika Prajñaparamita*, which can be seen as
a true Zen text:

Subhuti: How must a bodhisattva practice in order to see clearly that things do not have their own nature?

Buddha: Forms must be seen as devoid of the true nature of form; sensations must be seen as devoid of the true nature of sensation. It is the same concerning the other sense organs and their objects.

Subhuti: If things are devoid of true nature, how can the bodhisattva realize perfect wisdom?

Buddha: It is non-realization which is in the process of realizing perfect wisdom.

Subhuti: Why is this realization a non-realization?

Buddha: Because we cannot conceive wisdom nor the bodhisattva who practices wisdom, as we cannot conceive realization, the one who realizes, the methods of realization, or the means of realization. The realization of wisdom is therefore a non-realization in which all speculation is useless.

Subhuti: If this is so, how can a beginner realize wisdom?

Buddha: From the first moment of awareness, the bodhisattva must meditate on the inaccessible nature, or non-attainability [*anupalambha*], of things. While practicing the six paramitas, the bodhisattva must say to himself that there is nothing to be attained.

Subhuti: What is attainment? What is non-attainment?

Buddha: Where object and subject still exist, attainment exists. Where the object and subject cease to exist, non-attainment exists.

Subhuti: What is the subject-object and what is the non-subject-object?

Buddha: Where the distinction between eye and form, ear and sound, nose and smell, tongue and taste, body and sensation, cogitation and thought still exists; where the distinction between the person who realizes enlightenment and the enlightenment that is realized exists, the subject-object exists. Where there is no longer a distinction between eye and form, ear and sound, nose and smell, tongue and taste, body and sensation, cogitation and thought; where there is no longer the person who realizes enlightenment and the enlightenment realized, there there is no longer subject-object.

THE THREE GATES OF LIBERATION

The Ts'ao T'ung school, as we know, emphasizes the importance of non-attainment. This position reflects the spirit of the

Prajñaparamita. The principles of "meditation without subject" and "practice and enlightenment are one" certainly derive from the principle of non-attainment. It must be recognized here that the doctrine of non-attainment has as its origin the notion of *aimlessness (apranihita)* in early Buddhism. The *Digha Nikaya, Lalita Vistara, Abhidharmakosa Sastra, Vibhasa,* and *Visudhimagga* all speak of this in the context of the "three gates of liberation."

The three gates of liberation are *emptiness* (sunyata), *signlessness (animitta)*, and *aimlessness* (apranihita). *Emptiness* is the absence of permanent identity of things. *Signlessness* is the nature of non-conceptualization of things. *Aimlessness* is the attitude of someone who does not feel the need to run after anything, realize or obtain anything. It is, for example, not pursuing enlightenment as an object of knowledge. The Sanskrit word "apranihita" means "to put nothing in front of oneself." The *Vibhasa, Abhidharmakosa Sastra,* and *Visudhimagga* have the tendency to interpret aimlessness as non-desire; since things are impermanent, one must not run after them. For the same reason these texts interpret signlessness as the false value of data provided by the sense organs.

The three gates of liberation are therefore interpreted by the majority of early Buddhist texts from a moral rather than an epistemological point of view. In Mahayana Buddhism in general, and Zen in particular, a close relationship can be found among the three gates. Absence of an absolute identity in each thing (emptiness) is manifested by the non-conceptual (signlessness) knowledge in which a subject in quest of an object does not exist (aimlessness). In the true knowledge of reality, the distinction between subject and object, obtaining and obtained, no longer exists.

But if aimlessness means the cessation of the desire vis-à-vis impermanent things, it could be said that in this case the desire vis-à-vis liberation, or the desire for enlightenment, still exists, which is radically opposed to the idea of aimlessness in the *Prajñaparamita* and in Zen. Jacques Gernet, in the introduction to his translation of *Conversations with Master Shen Hui*,[3] speaks of the sudden enlightenment of Zen as being a special product of Chinese Zen Buddhism, which does not exist in Indian Buddhism. In my opinion, this is not correct. The notion of non-attainment in the *Prajñaparamita* was the basis for the doctrine of sudden enlightenment. The passages of the *Prajñaparamita* that we have cited clearly demonstrate this.

THE EIGHT NEGATIONS OF NAGARJUNA

In the second century C.E., Nagarjuna systematized *Prajñaparamita* thought. He compiled the *Mahaprajñaparamita Sastra*, the *Madhyamika Sastra*, and the *Dvadasanikaya Sastra*. His disciple, Arya Deva, compiled the *Sata Sastra* in the same line

[3] Published in Hanoi in 1949.

of thought. Nagarjuna's three texts later became the foundation of a Mahayana school called Madhyamika in India and San Lun in China. Candrakirti was the founder of the Madhyamika and Ki Tsang that of San Lun.

The method of the Madhyamika demonstrates the absurdity and uselessness of concepts and aims at showing the reality of emptiness as dealt with by the *Prajñaparamita*. It is not a linguistic philosophy, a simple play of words, or an intellectual exercise. The aim of the Madhyamika is to reduce all concepts to absurdity in order to open the door of non-conceptual knowledge. It is not the intention of the Madhyamika to propose a view of reality in order to set it up in opposition to other views of reality. *All views*, according to the Madhyamika, are erroneous, because the views are not reality. The Madhyamika is, therefore, proposed as a method and not as a doctrine. This makes the Madhyamika the legitimate heir to the *Prajñaparamita* thought.

In his *Madhyamika Sastra*, Nagarjuna proposes the following eight negations:

There is no generation;
There is no destruction;
There is no continuation;
There is no interruption;
There is no unity;
There is no plurality;
There is no arriving;
There is no departing.

This is the negation of the eight fundamental concepts through which reality is habitually considered. Other concepts derived from it, such as cause/effect, time/space, subject/object, etc., are also analyzed and finally rejected by Nagarjuna as simply products of discriminative knowledge. When speaking of generation, for example, one also speaks of the object generated; but if one goes in search of this object, one does not find it. Generation is not possible without an object that is generated. Nothing generates itself, says Nagarjuna, because generation as such does not exist. To demonstrate this, Nagarjuna poses the question: before the effect E is produced as a function of the cause C, does the effect E already exist within the cause C?

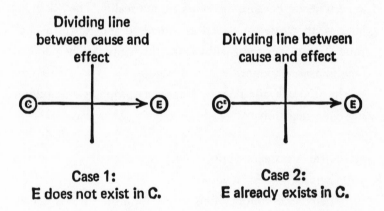

If we reply (case 1) that the effect E does not exist in the cause C, Nagarjuna demonstrates to us that in this case generation is not possible. Indeed, if there is no relation between C and E, if E does not exist in C, it is impossible that E should arise from C. A chick cannot be born of a table; a chick is born from an egg. If we reply (case 2) that E already exists in cause C, Nagarjuna demonstrates to us that, in this case, E has no need of being generated since it already exists. The relation between an egg and a chick is not a relation of cause and effect; it is of becoming and not generation. The concept of *generation* is thus rendered absurd. In the process of his analysis, the nature of impermanence, not-self, and emptiness of what we believe to be the object of generation and of destruction can be seen.

THE MIDDLE WAY

All concepts are destroyed in the same way by Nargarjuna, who takes every precaution necessary to avoid replacing one concept with another. In the process of analyzing the concept *generation*, for example, the concepts "becoming" and "non-production" are brought forth. Both these concepts must also succumb to Nagarjuna's dialectic. This dialectic aims at combating concepts in such a way that the concepts that are diametrically opposed to them cannot be used. For this reason it is called "The Middle Way." The term "middle" does not signify a synthesis between opposing concepts, such as "being" and "nonbeing," "generation" and "destruction." It signifies the transcendence of all concepts.

This dialectic is also expressed in the principle of the *two truths:* absolute truth (*paramartha satya*) and relative truth (*sam-vritti satya*). In its pure form, presented by an enlightened person, dialectic is absolute truth. Seized by concepts, it becomes relative truth. To render it absolute once more, it is necessary to take a new step; and if it is still conceptualized, another step must be taken in order to bring it back to its pure, original form.

Conceptual Description (relative truth)	Non-Conceptual Description in a dialectic form (absolute truth)
Being	Nonbeing
Being and nonbeing	Neither Being nor nonbeing
Being and nonbeing – neither Being nor nonbeing	Neither nonbeing nor non-nonbeing
Neither nonbeing nor non-nonbeing	Neither "neither nonbeing" nor "nor non-nonbeing," etc.

According to the principles of the "three gates of liberation," negation, therefore, has the role of breaking down concepts to the point where the practitioner comes to rid himself of all discrimination and penetrates undiscriminated reality. Dialectic aims at producing a transforming crisis and not at expounding a truth. In this close relationship between the language and attitude of Zen, Prajñaparamita thought and Madhyamika thought can be clearly seen.

Zen Masters do not use dialectic in the way that Nagarjuna does, but their words, acts, and looks also have the function of combating concepts, of producing crises, and of creating conditions that arrive at releasing the vision of reality. If we were to spend our days in a Zen monastery studying Prajñaparamita and Madhyamika texts, there would not be enough time to practice Zen. But these texts are available, even in the monastery, and can be consulted at any time.

THE VIJÑANAVADA SCHOOL

The Vijñanavada school, which benefits considerably from the researches of the Sarvastivada school and inherits from it to some extent, also deals with the problem of tathata, as did Prajñaparamita thought, but from the phenomenological view. The most fundamental texts of the Vijñanavada school are the *Sandhinirmocana Sutra*, which appeared during the middle of the second century, and the *Lankavatara Sutra*, which appeared during the beginning of the third century C.E. According to Daisetz Teitaro Suzuki, the *Lankavatara* is not a true Vijñanavada text, but a Zen text. The reason for this, he says, is that it is the only text transmitted by Bodhidharma, the First Zen Ancestor, to his disciple Hui Ko, and, further, the text emphasizes the importance of the inner spiritual experience of Buddha and of reaching enlightenment. But, in fact, nearly all Buddhist texts speak about this spiritual experience and about reaching enlightenment. It cannot be said that the *Prajñaparamita* texts are not *basic* Zen texts; on the contrary, the

Vajracchedika (Diamond Cutter) and the *Hridaya* (Heart) are the
two most popular *Prajñaparamita* texts among Zen practitioners. The fact that Bodhidharma transmitted to Hui Ko the
Lankavatara clarifies only one thing for us: the *Lankavatara* was
the favorite text of Bodhidharma.

The *Lankavatara* can be considered as a basic text for
Zen Buddhism, as Suzuki thought, but it is at the same
time the basic text of the Vijñanavada school. This demonstrates that there is a close relationship between the Vijñanavada and Zen, just as there is between the Prajñaparamita and
Zen.

CLASSIFICATION OF THE DHARMAS

The Vijñanavada classifies dharmas (things) into five groups:

1. Phenomena of mind (*citta*), of which there are
   eight.
2. Phenomena of states of mind (*citta sika*), of which
   there are fifty-one.
3. Physical and physiological phenomena (*rupa*), of
   which there are eleven.
4. Relational phenomena (*citta viprayutasamsaka*), of
   which there are twenty-four.
5. Unconditioned phenomena (*asankrta*), of which
   there are six.

In all, there are one hundred dharmas. The last category groups the dharmas under consideration as unconditioned, and distinguishes: (1) unconditioned space, i.e., that which is neither created nor destroyed by conditions; (2) the unconditioned acquired by enlightenment; (3) the nature of the unconditioned, which has nothing to do with enlightenment; (4) the unconditioned that is freedom from all pleasure and pain; (5) the unconditioned that is the cessation of all thought and sensation; (6) the unconditioned of tathata.

It should be noticed at this point that tathata is also considered to be a dharma. If one calls "all that can be conceptualized" to be a dharma, why can tathata, which transcends all concepts, also be considered as a dharma? The Vijñanavada replies: "Tathata and all other dharmas cannot be conceptualized. It is only by convention or expediency that one uses these representations."

The *Trimsika Vijñaptimatrata* of Vasubandhu begins with this declaration concerning these representations:

It is because of the presupposed existence of permanent identities and of dharmas that possess this permanent identity that so many diverse representations are manifest. All these representations come from conscious knowledge [*vijñana*].

Conscious Knowledge

Thus, the recognition of one hundred dharmas divided into five groups is only an acceptance of the presupposition that dharmas exist. This acceptance serves as a means for the beginning of the exposition of the Vijñanavada doctrine. This already emphasizes the difference between the methodology of Vijñanavada and that of the Sarvastivada. According to Vijñanavada, all sensation, perception, thought, or knowledge is manifested from the store consciousness, which is called *alayavijñana*. In its non-conceptualized nature, alayavijñana is tathata or "wisdom of the great and perfect mirror."

There are in all eight kinds of conscious knowledge (vijñanas), which are classified in three categories:

1. *Vijñana of knowledge of objects (vijñaptirvisaya)*, which concerns sight, touch, hearing, taste, and smell, and the *manovijñana*, which is the center of sensations, perceptions, and thoughts.
2. *Vijñana of the activity of thought (manas)*, center of the discrimination self/not-self and of reflections.
3. *Vijñana of the base (alaya)*, the base of the manifestation of all knowledge, subject and object.

The *Mahayana Sraddhotpada Sastra* says about the alaya:

> True mind [ultimate reality] can be seen from two
> sides: the side of birth/death [phenomenal] and the
> side of true nature [tathata]. Phenomena come from
> the "tathata"; phenomena are neither the replica of
> "tathata" nor different from it: "alaya" means the basis
> of conservation and manifestation of all the dharmas;
> i.e., the "tathata."

All the vijñanas, all sensations, perceptions, and cogita-
tions contain in themselves at the same time their subject and
their object of knowledge. When the eye is opposite a flower,
one can say that the eye and the flower are dharmas that can
exist separately; *but when "seeing" occurs, the subject and object of the
seeing exist at the same time in the sensation.* The flower is not the
object seen. The object of the seeing is found in the seeing
itself, and cannot exist independently of the subject of the
sensation.

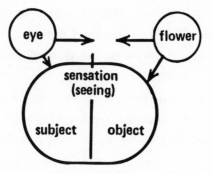

This figure shows us that when sensation occurs, the first phase, which is contact between the physiological phenomenon (eye) and the physical phenomenon (flower), has already passed in order to arrive at the second phase, which is the sensation (seeing). This underlines another difference between the phenomenological style of the Vijñanavada and the Sarvastivada's tendency toward pluralistic realism. Does *the image of the flower* in the sensation faithfully reflect the *flower* in reality? This is an important question. The relation between the reality of the flower and the sensation that arises from it is another subject posed by the Vijñanavada.

The first point reveals that the world of sensations and of concepts is only the world of vijñana (conscious knowledge). The object of vijñanas is only the object of knowledge. One can then wonder whether the physiological and physical conditions, according to which the vijñanas are produced, truly exist at all. The Vijñanavada tells us they exist, as an object of alaya, and one can call them the "world of reality in itself." The role of alaya is to maintain all the dharmas and to make them appear. Alaya is also defined as *sarvabijaka* (all the seeds). The word "alaya" implies to conserve and to maintain. Though considered as a vijñana, alaya does not function as do the manovijñana or the manas on the discrimination of subject and object, self and not-self.

In the case of pure sensation, where the discrimination of subject/object does not exist, the "world of reality in itself" is revealed. This world of reality in itself is tathata, the true nature of alaya. If the vijñanas are separated from the discrimination of subject/object, they become wisdom (*jñanas*) and perfect revelation of reality in itself.

METHOD OF VIJÑANAVADA

Each vijñana consists of three parts: subject (*darsanabhaga*), object (*nimittabhaga*), and true nature (*svasamvittibhaga*).

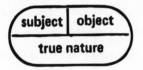

Each sensation, perception, and thought also possess these three parts. The notion of three parts shows that the Vijñanavada emphasizes the ontological problem. The part called "true nature" is considered to be the basis of reality, the essence of vijñana and tathata. The first two parts are only the manifestation of tathata. As each drop of water in the ocean is salty, each dharma is a manifestation of tathata. Seeing reality does not come about by pinning things down, but by seeing into their true nature.

What is the methodology proposed by the Vijñanavada?

First of all the importance of non-duality must be recognized. Things depend on each other in being produced; they do not possess an independent true identity. This is called the *interdependent nature (paratantra)* of things. All knowledge not based on the principle of paratantra is incorrect. It does not reflect reality. Indeed, it carries with it this illusion-imagination which is called vikalpa. Vikalpa cuts reality into separate pieces, giving them each separate identities. Vikalpa discriminates. If vikalpa is destroyed, knowledge becomes pure and able to reveal tathata. Things will then be presented in their thusness. They will reveal their nature of *nispanna* (perfect reality). Knowledge, being pure, is called wisdom (jñana).

In reality vikalpa, paratantra, and nispanna are only states of knowledge. When knowledge is vikalpa, the object of knowledge is also vikalpa. When knowledge is clarified by the paratantra, the object of knowledge is revealed in its paratantra nature. When knowledge is absolutely pure, the object of knowledge is nispanna. Once again we see that the subject and object of knowledge are one.

Having dealt with these three natures (*tri-svabhavas*) of dharmas, the Vijñanavada tells us that these three natures do not truly exist. Take, for example, the vikalpa nature (illusion-imagination) of things. This nature is only a kind of illusory veil through which things are seen. It is the same for the paratantra and nispanna natures. As things do not have true identity, they cannot possess any "nature."

The Vijñanavada therefore establishes the principle of three non-natures (*tri-nisvabhavatas*) to combat the principle of three natures which was first established to guide people in the way of the purification of knowledge. This method makes us think of the method of Madhyamika, which uses concepts to destroy concepts. At the same time it shows us that the Vijñanavada is closely connected to the method of Zen. Absolute reality, according to Vijñanavada, cannot be described by the three natures or by the three non-natures, or by any other concept. This is because it is tathata, because it is the absolute truth of the dharmas (*dharmanam paramarthas*), absolute truth that is revealed only by enlightenment.

Just like the *Prajñaparamita* and Zen, the Vijñanavada emphasizes the importance of *non-attainment* in the process of purification of knowledge. Vasubandhu says in his *Trimsika:*

As long as the vijñana does not wish to remain in peace in its non-dualistic nature, the roots of discrimination between subject and object are still there, indestructible.

When the practitioner places in front of himself something that he considers as the true nature of vijñana [*vijñaptimatra-svabhava*], he is still not in the heart of the true nature of vijñana, because he still distinguishes subject and object.

When, faced with the object of knowledge, he does not consider it as an object of his own realization, the practitioner begins to live in peace in the true nature of vijñana, because he has rendered the dualistic discrimination immanent.

This reality, which can neither be conceived nor
obtained, is transcendental wisdom.

ALAYA AS THE BASIS

The true nature of vijñana, of which Vasubandhu speaks, is
none other than tathata, the "illuminating nature of knowledge." In the state of enlightenment, the five vijñanas of sensation become "the wisdom of the miraculous powers"; manovijñana becomes "the wisdom of marvelous inspection";
manas become "the wisdom of non-discriminating nature"; and
alaya becomes "the wisdom of the great and perfect mirror."

Zen Buddhism does not enter the realm of analysis and
discussion as does the Vijñanavada, but it brings out its spirit
in a profound way. The notion of alaya can throw a great deal
of light on the mechanism of enlightenment in Zen. Alaya is
the profound base of life and the psyche while the manovijñana and the manas are only reflecting elements, ideas,
and concepts. From the phenomenological point of view,
alaya is the basis of being and nonbeing. It conserves and
maintains the energies and essences that are manifested in the
dharmas. These energies and essences are called seeds (bijas).
Manas and manovijñana are manifested on the basis of alaya.
The roots coming from their errors are thrust into alaya and
are called *anusaya*. The practitioner of meditation on paratan-

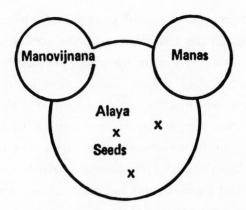

tra (interdependent nature of things) brings about changes at the heart of alaya, and these changes transform and neutralize the anusaya roots. Enlightenment is the fruit of this transformation, called *asrayaparavrtti*. According to Huian Tsang, the word signifies transformation (*paravrtti*) and support (*asraya*). To transform is not to destroy. The support is here paratantra. Using the principle of paratantra as a basis, one transforms the seeds and roots of ignorance into seeds and roots of enlightenment. This transformation does not come about only in manas and manovijñana, it comes about in the heart of alaya itself. When alaya is enlightened, manas and manovijñana are also enlightened.

To the enlightened person, flowers and grass, mountains and rivers, are no longer given as vikalpa images but are given in the reality they acquire in the "wisdom of marvelous inspection." The expression "wisdom of non-discriminating nature" indicates the ability of an enlightened person to penetrate to the heart of reality itself, without being paralyzed by duality.

The efforts of manovijñana alone do not culminate in enlightenment. In the first place, since the very basis of manovijñana is alaya, a genuine transformation must be realized
at the heart of alaya; second, reality itself is not revealed in
manovijñana, which still clings to dualism. For this reason,
alaya itself must be put into action in order to transform the
seeds (bijas) of the *two attachments* (the errors concerning self/
not-self, subject/object). Each moment in which manovijñana
is enlightened by paratantra and nispanna is a moment of
mindfulness, a moment of Zen, in which all vikalpa images are
absent.

THE PROCESS OF ENLIGHTENMENT

Let us read the following important passage in the *Lankavatara
Sutra*, in order to understand clearly the process of enlightenment of Zen and Vijñanavada:

> Mahamati, the five kinds of dharmas are:
> representations [*nimitta*], names [*nama*], discrimination
> [*vikalpa*], thusness [*tathata*] and true wisdom [*samya-
> jñana*].
>
> All forms, colors, and images, etc., are called rep-
> resentations [nimitta].
>
> From these representations concepts are formed,

such as the concept of the base on the model "this is this," "this is not that," etc. It is this which is called names [nama]. "Conscious-knowledge" and its functions, which gives rise to these concepts, is called discrimination [vikalpa].

These representations and concepts are not true things that can be obtained; they are only the product of discrimination. The true nature of things, liberated from this discrimination, is called thusness [tathata].

Mahamati, these are the characteristics of thusness: reality, exactitude, ultimate end, true nature, foundation, and non-attainment.

The Buddhas and myself have realized and expounded thusness.

All those who are capable of making good use of this exposition in order to penetrate into thusness can transcend concepts of continuity and discontinuity, get rid of discrimination-imagination, and reach the spiritual experience of self-realization, an experience unknown to philosophers, Sravakas, and Pratyekabuddhas. This is called true wisdom [samyajñana].

Mahamati, the five kinds of dharmas that I have just expounded to you imply the essential doctrine of the three natures, the eight vijñanas, and the two stages of *nairatmyas* (no true identity).

Mahamati, you must use your ability to realize these dharmas. Once you have realized them, your mind will be confirmed; nothing will be able to disturb you.

By way of illustration, we can use a circle with C at its center. The circle, perfectly round, symbolizes the reality of

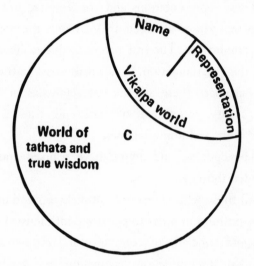

tathata, which reveals only the true non-discriminating and non-dualistic wisdom. In the unenlightened state, however, what we take for our world of reality is only the world of discrimination (vikalpa), which is manifested on the tathata basis. In this world of discrimination, subject and object, representation and name, are revealed. By penetrating through skillful means, we come back to the world of tathata and true wisdom. But that does not imply the disappearance of the world of phenomena. What disappears is discrimination-imagination. The world of phenomena is revealed in true wisdom without being veiled by vikalpa. *The world of phenomena is but one with the world of tathata in the same way that waves cannot be separated from the water.*

The passage quoted from the *Lankavatara* now becomes clearer. The expression "penetration by skillful means" makes us think of the *Sraddhotpada Sastra,* in which Asvaghosa speaks of the efforts of penetration by a clever use of words and concepts. In Buddhism, the language of the enlightened person aims at expounding the way of realizing tathata. This language, which has its source in wisdom that transcends words and concepts, must, however, use words and concepts. When we reach absolute reality while using this language of words and concepts, we practice what the *Lankavatara* calls "penetration by skillful means."

Although Zen declares that it is not based on words and concepts, it in fact manipulates words and concepts in order to reveal the reality that transcends words and concepts. The master achieves success or failure according to whether his disciple can or cannot "penetrate by skillful means" when the master's pole is held out to her. If the disciple is attached to the word of her master in the way of vikalpa, the release of enlightenment will be impossible for her. It must be clearly understood that though Zen masters may not encourage their disciples to spend their time studying the Madhyamika and the Vijñanavada, it is not because these doctrines contradict Zen; in fact, they can very well illustrate the development of Zen. *But Zen is not the study of Zen; Zen is life.* Zen is direct contact with reality. The Madhyamika and Vijñanavada doctrines can explain many things, but they do not put the practitioner in direct contact with living reality. Zen can only be lived and experienced. As Master Tue Trung Thuong Si said, "This marvelous piece must be played." What is the good of discussing a musical masterpiece? It is the performance that counts.

VI

THE REGENERATION

OF HUMANITY

MONASTIC LIFE

Zen monastic life is very well organized. The tradition is the same today as it was in the eighth century when Master Po Chang set down the monastic code that carries his name. The monastery where he lived was on the Ta Hiong Mountain at Hong Chou in the province of Kiang Hi. The name of the mountain was later changed to Po Chang.

Po Chang's rules are a synthesis of the spirit of the early Buddhist and Mahayana disciplines. The monastic tradition of the Zen school began to be distinct and independent of the monastic tradition of the Vinaya school of that time.

Each monastery is placed under the direction of a Superior, *vien chu* or *giam vien*. The monk who has the role of administrative director is called *tri su*, and he is responsible for the monastery as if it were a community or an organization. The monk *tri vien* has charge of the garden and grounds, the *thu kho* that of the kitchen, the *tri tang* that of the library, the *tri dien* and the *huong dang* that of the sanctuary. The *tri khach* looks after the visitors, monks, and laypeople; the *duy na* is in charge of the recitation meetings and ceremonies; and the *tri chung* is charged with problems concerning relations between members of the community. There are some jobs that are done by

everyone in turn; the monks who are responsible for them
during the day are called the *tri nhat*. The young and the
novices (*sramanera*) fill the role of *thi gia* (attendants) in order to
help the high monks in their daily existence, and to learn from
them the way to conduct themselves in monastic life.

Twice a month all the monks meet in the Buddha Hall for
the *bo tat* ceremony, a review of the observance of the *bhikshu*
rules, of which there are two hundred and fifty, and of the
fifty-eight bodhisattva rules. Novices do not participate in the
recitation of these rules. They have their own novitiate rules,
of which there are ten, and their manual of conduct to recite
together in another room in the monastery. The six principles
of living in harmony, known as "the Six Concords," are also
recited:

1. To live together in the same conditions.
2. To observe the same rules.
3. To speak carefully to avoid dispute.
4. To share one's goods.
5. To share different points of view.
6. To create harmony of opinion in order to maintain
   the *joie de vivre* of the community.

The monks get up at four o'clock in the morning to the
sound of the *bao chung* bell. They have fifteen minutes to wash,
dress, and make their beds. Then they gather in the Meditation Hall and practice sitting meditation.

A monk stands by the bao chung bell and chants the

meditation chant, accompanied by the sound of this bell. It is a prelude chant:

> The fifth division of the night has already begun and the door to reality is open.
>
> I wish the whole world were on the path of wisdom, that each person penetrate deeply the teachings of the three vehicles and realize the harmony of the two truths, and that the sun of great realization rise and dispel all clouds of darkness.

The great bell is sounded regularly and slowly during the meditation period (*toa thien*).

After toa thien everyone assembles in the Buddha Hall for sutra recitation.

Breakfast is normally a bowl of rice, sometimes mixed with beans. It is eaten with pickled vegetables and soy sauce. Silence is maintained during eating; when the meal is finished, the *Prajñaparamita Hridaya* sutra is recited.

After breakfast each monk goes about his task. The housework is done, the sanctuary floor is washed; some monks work in the garden or in the fields, carry water, or look for firewood.

At 11:30 A.M. there is a short rest. Lunch is at midday and is the principal meal. When the bao chung bell is invited to sound, each monk washes and dresses in the *ao trang*, then goes in procession to the dining hall and sits upright on his seat in front of his bowl. The meal proceeds according to a ceremony; body and mind are fixed on the content of the meal. In the afternoon from two-thirty until five-thirty, there is another work period. The evening meal, if there is one, consists of rice soup and the leftovers from lunch.

A period for sutra recitation begins at seven in the evening. After eight comes the time of study and practice of sitting meditation. Bedtime follows the end of the last meditation period. Anyone who wishes may continue to meditate late into the night.

THE RETREATS

Each year, from the fifteenth of the fourth lunar month to the fifteenth of the seventh month, the *ket ha* season is organized. During this period one does not leave the monastery and intensively practices toa thien. Monks who live alone in distant pagodas return to their monasteries in order to participate in the ket ha season. This is a period of concentrated study and practice.

Sometimes *ket dong* seasons, which also last three months, are organized in the winter. These allow whoever could not leave his pagoda or community during the summer ket ha to participate in ket dong.

Outside the collective meditation hall, which can sometimes hold up to several hundred monks, there also exist little Zen huts for one person called *that* or *coq*. In Vietnam, especially in the southern part, many of these little Zen huts are found. The climate is warm in the southern region, and it is ample protection to construct small huts with bamboo and coconut palm leaves in a simple way. A Zen practitioner can remain in his coq three years, or one year, or three months, according to his liking. A novice is appointed to assist him during this period.

The period during which a Zen monk intends to be alone in his coq (*nhap that*) is truly a period of absolute retreat. The monk does not leave the vicinity of the coq. The novice who attends him maintains connections between the monastery and the coq; he gets water, rice, vegetables, fruit, etc. The monk in retreat may do his own cooking. In his coq there is only a bed (which also serves as a meditation seat), a table, a lamp, a towel, a toothbrush, and some sutras. The monk, during this solo retreat, rarely speaks or does not speak at all. His assistant must be very attentive; he must know what his master needs, and make his life as comfortable as possible. While assisting a master in retreat, a novice can learn many things in silence.

For the most part, the ket ha, ket dong, and nhap that periods are devoted to the practice of toa thien. The practitioner sits on his cushion in the lotus posture, the right foot placed on the left thigh and left foot placed on the right thigh. He holds his head up and his spine straight, keeps his eyes down, and places the left hand on the right hand. The lotus posture is a very stable and energizing position. If beginners feel some pain in this position, they can begin by practicing the half-lotus position, with just the right leg placed on the left thigh, or vice versa.

After several hours stationary in the lotus posture, the practitioner may get up and walk in *kinh hanh*, a very slow walk in the meditation hall or around the coq. If the toa thien is practiced collectively, the time of kinh hanh will be fixed in advance. One walks in file, very slowly, silently, with eyes lowered, several times around the meditation hall in a clock-wise direction. Mindfulness is maintained while walking, tak-ing one step with the left foot while breathing in and one step with the right foot while breathing out. Alternating toa thien and kinh hanh ensures that the blood circulation is maintained and eases the pain in the legs.

But mindfulness is not only practiced during toa thien and kinh hanh. It is necessary to learn to remain in mindfulness even while working in the garden, sweeping the courtyard, washing clothes, or washing the dishes. Many Zen masters have come to enlightenment during their daily work. It is essential that a Zen practitioner be able to live mindfully in each moment of the day. *There is no enlightenment outside of daily life.*

The Encounter

From time to time interviews are organized during which the disciple finds himself face to face with his teacher. He tells his teacher about his experiences, his difficulties, and his doubts. He may also present his view of Zen in order to get instructions. These meetings are called *tham thien* (Japanese: *sanzen*) or Zen encounters. Questions and answers may sometimes be expressed very energetically. The disciple then has the opportunity to present himself and his individual case. Encounters of this sort, as well as impromptu encounters between the master and a group of monks in a corridor or in a garden, are called *tieu tham* or small encounters. The encounters that take place at fixed times, in which the whole assembly participates, are called *dai tham* or great encounters.

The exchange of questions and answers during these great encounters may have the appearance of formidable confrontations. A monk presents himself to the master before the entire assembly and exposes himself to a severe test. The master uses questions, sometimes even yells or physical blows, in order to put the disciple to the test. Everyone attends as a witness to the scene, in a state of tension that arouses great mindfulness in them. Monks who voluntarily offer themselves to the test are described as "entering into combat" (*xuat tran*).

Senior monks sometimes leave the monastery in order to live in a private hut, to become masters in a new monastery, or to go on a pilgrimage. What has been described here has been very general, and of course is the same practice for nuns. Plum Village, where I now live and practice in France, is a community of both monks and nuns, living in separate hamlets.

The Role of the Laity

Zen, however, does not belong to monks only. Everyone can study and practice it. Many laymen have been recognized as illustrious Zen masters. The laity are related to the monasteries by the material support they provide, as it sometimes happens that the labor of the monks is not sufficient to ensure the upkeep of the monastery. The laity are also related to the monasteries by their participation in the construction of temples and sanctuaries and by their cultural activities; for example, the printing and publishing of sutras and scriptural works by monks. A good number of monasteries each month organize *bat quan trai gioi* for laymen who wish to live for twenty-four or forty-eight hours in a monastery exactly like monks. Places are reserved for them for these periods of bat quan trai gioi, during which they practice Zen under the direction of monks.

It is through the close interaction of the laity and the monks that the essence of Zen penetrates social life. Zen influences poetry, painting, architecture, and music. The traditions of flower arrangement, tea ceremony, calligraphy, Chinese ink painting, and watercolor have their source in the spiritual reality of Zen. Zen is not only reflected in the technique of art but also by the essence of the art. The technique reflects the self-mastery of the artist, while the content reflects the spiritual understanding of the artist. The arts are the connecting link between the spiritual world of Zen and the everyday world of society.

ZEN AND THE WORLD OF TODAY

Our picture of an enlightened person is of someone very free who possesses spiritual strength and is not pushed around by the currents of society. The practitioner, once enlightened, sees herself in her true nature, knows herself, and possesses a clear view of reality—the reality of her being and of the social situation. This vision is the most precious fruit Zen can offer. The enlightened person's way of being is the most fundamental and beneficent contribution to society and all life that she can make. Zen is a living tradition that produces stable, healthy, and balanced people. The arts and thought that have their source in the enlightenment of Zen also possess this vitality and clear-sighted serenity.

Contemporary man is dragged along in a producing and consuming treadmill to the point where he begins to become a part of the machine and loses mastery of himself. Daily life dissipates our spirit, eats up our time, and thus does not leave the opportunity to become aware of ourselves or return to our deeper self. Accustomed as we are to being constantly "occupied," if these occupations should be taken from us, we find ourselves empty and abandoned. Still, we refuse to confront ourself and instead go off in search of friends, to mix in with the crowd, to listen to the radio or to the television, to get rid of this impression of emptiness.

Present-day life, agitated to the extreme, makes us so easily irritated. Emotions overwhelm us many times a day; in fact, they dominate and possess us. If we are no longer ourselves, how can we say that it is we who live and decide our life?

Life today is organized according to "reason." We participate in life with only part of our being—our intellect, our manovijñana. The other half, deeper and more important, is the store consciousness, the foundation of the roots of our being. This part cannot be analyzed by reason or even by the manovijñana itself. Man today loves reason. He trusts his rationality so much that he is uprooted from his true being. From this comes the feeling of alienation from which he suffers and through this, little by little, his humanity becomes more and more mechanical.

The revolt of the 1960s and 1970s was a manifestation of our desire to recapture our human spirit. If we are unable to create a new path by which to discover our true nature, the human race may be condemned to disappear. Never in history have we had to face such potentially calamitous dangers. We are no longer able to control the situation. The economic, political, and military systems we have established have turned against us and imposed themselves on us, and we have become increasingly "dehumanized."

FUTURE PERSPECTIVES

Let us consider, for example, the problem of food. The world population is presently almost 6 billion, and the majority of the members of the human family go to bed hungry every night. The Third World War will not be unleashed by the great powers; it will break out first in the zones of famine and oppression. Famine and political oppression are the most profound causes for all war. Today all wars (Vietnam, the Persian Gulf) have an international character; the great powers are engaged in them to a greater or lesser extent because their influence and their prestige are tied in large measure to these wars. People on all sides trembled during the Cuban Missile Crisis. A world war can explode at any moment. A false alarm can create a complete panic. Will we possess the coolness necessary to control the situation? It would take only 250 atomic bombs to destroy the continent and people of North America. We *still* possess enough nuclear bombs to destroy everyone on Earth many times, and the buttons to trigger these weapons are in the reach of human beings.

Pesticides and defoliants, used in the wars and also in agriculture, have affected the ecological system of the entire Earth. According to a UNESCO study, pelicans are becoming extinct along the California coast. The eggs in all but five of twelve hundred pelican nests were infected by DDT and could not hatch. The conclusion of this report was, "Man will perhaps perish by his own fault."

Paul Erlich has stated, "Theoretically the new techniques of agriculture should be able to increase the production of food to feed seven billion or more people, but practically speaking, it is impossible." Sterling Bunnell added, "If we try to slow down famine by applying all the techniques that we know, such as the use of chemical fertilizers and insecticides, we would completely contaminate our biological environment. Nothing could survive in it, including man."

The separation between the rich and the underdeveloped countries continues to get greater and greater, and we cannot expect this separation to disappear in the near future. The debts that poor countries have to pay to the rich are greater each year than the sums they receive in aid to help them develop economically. The lack of capital, the lack of political stability, and the necessity to resist exploitation carried on by the great economic powers increase the difficulties and obstacles that the poorer countries meet on the way to liberation. At the same time, the affluent societies of the West consume the vast majority of the Earth's resources and pollute the Earth and its atmosphere by this consumption. The United States, for example, represents about 5 percent of the world's population; but it consumes nearly 40 percent of the world's resources.

This disequilibrium makes the situation more and more dangerous. Professor C. P. Snow has predicted oceans of famine zones within decades. War, in such circumstances, cannot be avoided. Scientists, historians, and sociologists have sounded the alarm, but our societies do not seem to change.

We continue our daily lives contributing to the maintenance and consolidation of the machinery of production and consumption. We eat, drink, work, and distract ourselves, as if nothing is going to happen.

IS AWAKENING POSSIBLE?

The problem that faces us is the problem of *awakening*. What we lack is not an ideology or a doctrine that will save the world. What we lack is *mindfulness of what we are, of what our situation really is*. We need to wake up in order to rediscover our human sovereignty. We are riding a horse that is running out of control. The way of salvation is a new culture in which human beings are encouraged to rediscover their deepest nature.

Zen, as all other living spiritual traditions of the East or West, has contributed to the elevation of the spiritual life, while clarifying the way of thought, art, and culture. But Zen in Asia is also degenerating under the forces of technological civilization. The development of technology in the Western countries created the need to conquer African and Asian countries in order to ensure the possession of markets and industrial material. And the wars of liberation continue. War absorbs the energies of so many nations and aggravates the problem of hunger, already difficult to resolve because of rapid population growth. All this turns society and the structure of its moral values upside down.

The Zen tradition has also been shaken. In Vietnam, for example, the majority of Zen monasteries situated in distant regions in the mountains were destroyed during the war or afterward under the Communist regime. The government formed its own Buddhist church to control the practice of Buddhism in the country and continues to arrest Buddhists and others who call for the free practice of religion. In China, socialism has mobilized the mass of the people to realize national goals and in part to increase the army. The development of Japan's economy has made Japan into a Western-like nation, in which many of its spiritual values have given way to rampant materialism. The temples and monasteries must also participate in the present economic way of life and be based upon the present social needs of producing and consuming in order to exist. They can no longer play their role of spiritual leadership, as in the past. Zen is threatened on the very ground on which it was born and developed.

The West began to learn about Zen when it was already on its way to disintegration in Asia. Many of those in the West who appreciate Zen have had enough of the material civilization and the rationalist way. Technological civilization, based on logic and science, has reached its culmination, and has begun to produce crises and revolts. In this situation Zen appears as something fresh and comforting. Paradoxically, at the same time, the citizens of the countries of the Zen tradition are turning toward a life of material comfort and subscribing to policies of intensive industrialization of their countries. Their time and energies are almost completely devoted to it, and this is the reason why things like Zen can no longer continue to be important. The East, like the West, is witnessing a spiritual bankruptcy. The destruction of the human race can only be avoided by finding a new cultural direction in which the spiritual dimension plays the role of guide.

What we need is not another doctrine, but an awakening that can restore our spiritual strength. What made Mahatma Gandhi's struggle a great success was not a doctrine—not even the doctrine of nonviolence—but Gandhi himself, his way of being. A lot is written today about the doctrine of nonviolence, and people everywhere are trying to apply it. But they cannot rediscover the vitality that Gandhi had, because the "Gandhians" do not possess Gandhi's spiritual strength. They have faith in his doctrine but cannot set into motion a movement of great solidarity because none of them possess the spiritual force of a Gandhi and therefore cannot produce sufficient compassion and sacrifice.

If we continue to be dragged along by the machinery of producing and consuming, it will be difficult to build our spiritual strength. Gandhi dressed simply, walked on foot, and fed himself with frugality. The simplicity of his life is witness not only to his emancipation with regard to conditioning by material things, but also to great spiritual strength. The point of departure for a new civilization must be our determination not to be colonized by material goods or to contribute to the system of producing and consuming. Those determined to struggle against the treadmill of producing and consuming and for the recovery of human nature must be regarded as the avant-garde of our generation. Many people who live in abundance have revolted against materialism for *the need to be a human being*. This is not a new view. It is one of the fundamental human needs, stifled by superficial accumulation. This need to be a human being is our greatest hope, the element that can give birth to a new civilization.

The first phase of this civilization must be to establish social conditions in which life can be lived in a human way. "Awakened" people are certainly going to form small communities where their material life will be simple and healthy, and time and energy will be devoted to spiritual concerns. These communities of mindful living will be like Zen monasteries with no dogma. In them, the sickness of the times will be cured and spiritual health will be renewed. Great art and thought will be produced.

In the East, Zen monasteries still exist and the influence of Zen remains in literature, art, and manners. But Westerners seem more interested in Zen than people in the East, who are more preoccupied with material development and industrialization. They have not tasted the bitterness of materialism and the inhuman nature of technological civilization. The rebirth of Buddhism in several Asian countries in the twentieth century has been indirectly due to the work of Western scholars who, by their studies and research, have manifested their admiration for Buddhist art and thought. It is they who have helped the Asians regain confidence in their own cultural heritage. The same is happening with Zen Buddhism. Because Westerners are interested in Zen, many Asians have returned to their spiritual tradition.

But even for enlightened persons, however determined they may be, it is difficult to go against the system. What must we do to prevent ourselves from being overtaken by the system? Precipitating political or economic conflict does not seem to be the answer.

Western men and women are turning toward the East to find new sources of inspiration. In Eastern spirituality is found that tendency toward universal harmony that refreshes the heart. The East, although poor, has not suffered from the levels of fanaticism and violence that the West has. But the East has been oppressed; the East has risen all ready to struggle against the West with arms that the West has used against it. This is why the West has had difficulty in establishing a dialogue with the East. In its effort to learn from the West the technology that will enable it to defend itself, the East knows that it must be modest, ready to gather what it does not know. But the majority of Westerners do not possess this virtue of modesty in their approach to the East. They are satisfied with their methodology and their principles, and they remain attached to criteria and values of their own civilization while desiring to know the East. They are afraid of losing their identity and this is the principal cause of their difficulties.

Western civilization has brought us to the edge of the abyss. It has transformed us into machines. The "awakening" of a few Westerners, their awareness of our real situation has freed them of their superiority complex. They are engaged in the search for new values.

On the other side, some Asians have come to the West to introduce Eastern spiritual traditions. The intention is noble, but the task difficult. Unless they have a deep understanding of Western culture and mentality, success will be difficult to obtain. There is the risk of simply imposing an Asian way of life on Westerners, who ultimately will find it difficult to sustain. Zen is not a collection of rituals; it is life. Westerners who live in different social circumstances from those of the East cannot merely imitate these Asian Buddhists. In the same way that Chinese Zen has Chinese characteristics, Western Zen must be Western in its form.

An effort is therefore necessary. The West must be willing to shed some of its ideas and preconceptions in order to be open to receiving a new experience. Easterners who intend to help their Western friends must also make the effort to understand the Western mentality and Western cultural and social circumstances. It is only through such mutual efforts and collaboration that Zen will become a living tradition in Western soil.

Zen is the way of realizing the "true person," as Lin Chi

said. But the West also has spiritual traditions, formed in the course of its history and aiming at realizing its own "true person." We must honor the best aspects of all traditions. The problem is that many of these spiritual sources, Western and Eastern, have dried up. Religious institutions worldwide have become more political than spiritual. Motivated by material and political interests, they are engaged in worldly conflicts and neglect their spiritual task.

Technological civilization continually creates new needs of consumption, most of which are not important. This civilization has also created suffering and tragedies. Religions must be conscious of our need to awaken to our true humanity. Churches must work to rebuild communities in which a sane and healthy life can be lived, realizing that true happiness does not rest in the consumption of goods paid for by suffering, famine, and death, but in a life enlightened by the insight into interbeing and the recognition of our deep responsibility to be true to ourselves and to help our neighbors.

VII

LESSONS IN EMPTINESS

*Forty-three Kung-Ans
with comments and verses
of Tran Thai Tong
(1218–77)*

Tran Thai Tong was the first king of the Tran Dynasty (1225–1400) in Vietnam. He practiced Zen while reigning. At forty-one years of age he gave up the throne to his son, Tran Hoang, and devoted himself to the full-time practice of Zen. He was the author of two books: the *Thien Tong Chi Nam* (*Guide to Zen*) and the *Khoa Hu* (*Lessons in Emptiness*). The forty-three kung-ans presented here are taken from this latter book.[1]

QUESTIONS AND ANSWERS
BY WAY OF INTRODUCTION

One day when the Emperor[2] was visiting the pagoda of Chan Giao, Tong Duc Thanh put this riddle to him: "The World-

---

[1] For more about Tran Thai Tong and this golden period of Vietnamese history, see Thich Nhat Hanh, *Hermitage Among the Clouds* (Berkeley: Parallax Press, 1993).

[2] Tran Thai Tong himself. These dialogues are reported by his disciples.

Honored One was already born in the palace of King Suddhodana, even before having left Tusita heaven; he had fulfilled
the vow to save all living beings, even before he left his
mother's womb. What is the meaning of this?"

The Emperor replied, "All rivers reflect the moon in their
water. Where there is no cloud, the blue sky is seen."

A monk asked, "Those not yet liberated need instruction.
What about those already liberated?"

The Emperor replied, "The clouds that form at the summit
of Nhac Mountain are pure white. The waters that flow into
the River Tieu are clear blue."

Another monk inquired, "When clouds arrive, the color of
the mountains becomes soft; when the clouds depart, the
grotto becomes lighter. Why is it said that the hidden and the
revealed are the same?"

The Emperor replied, "Is there no one besides my own
descendants who dares to walk blindfolded?"

A monk said, "The Way is one-pointed. All the enlightened beings are on the Way to the one true source. Why do
you think that only Lord Buddha can find the road?"

The Emperor replied, "Spring rain waters all the plants
equally, and yet the flowering branches are long or short."

❖ ❖ ❖

A monk asked, "Each person possesses his own perfectly enlightened nature. Why did the World-Honored One have to go into the forest to realize the Way?"

The Emperor replied, "Because of injustice, the sword is drawn from its sheath. Because of illness, medicines are taken out of their jars."

A monk said, "No longer allowing the dust to get into one's eyes; no longer bringing on the itch by scratching the skin: such is my vision of the Way. Do you think that I have got something?"

The Emperor replied, "Water that flows down the mountain does not think that it flows down the mountain. The cloud that leaves the valley does not think that it leaves the valley."

The monk remained silent. The Emperor continued, "Do not think that non-thinking itself is the Way. Non-thinking is very far from the Way."

The monk replied, "If it is really a question of non-thinking, how is one able to say that *it is far* or *near?*"

The Emperor said, "The water that flows down the mountain does not think that it flows down the mountain. The cloud that leaves the valley does not think that it leaves the valley."

1 .

The Case

The World-Honored One was already born in the palace of King Suddhodana, even before having left Tusita heaven; he had fulfilled the vow to save all living beings, even before he left his mother's womb.

Commentary

The identity of the knight is revealed even before his sword is drawn from the sheath.

Verse

A small child who does not possess
even the form of a body,
leaves his village at midnight for the first time.
Making his people cross the seas
and visit distant countries
without the help of either boat or raft,
he meets no obstacle.

2 .

Case

The World-Honored One had just been born. With one hand pointing to the sky, the other to the earth, he said: "In heaven and earth, I alone am the World-Honored One."

Commentary

But one white cloud passes by the grotto and a thousand birds stray far from their nest.

Verse

Siddhartha should have revealed his true identity
when he was born in Suddhodana's palace.
He took seven steps and, with his hands,
pointed to heaven and earth.
Because of this obscene gesture, who knows
how many disciples were lost?

3 .

Case

The World-Honored One holds up a flower to the assembly. Mahakasyapa's face is transformed, and he smiles.

Commentary

Open your eyes and look carefully. A thousand mountain
ranges separate the one who reflects from the one who is truly
present.

Verse

While looking at the flower
that the World-Honored One raised in his hand,
Mahakasyapa found himself suddenly at home.
To call that "transmission of the essential Dharma"
is to say that, for him alone,
the chariot shaft is adequate transport.

4 .

Case

A philosopher asked the Buddha to neither speak nor be
silent.

Commentary

Only my own descendants
would dare to walk blindfolded.

Verse

Is it known how difficult it is
to shut the prison door?
Words and speech disappear.
No support remains.

If it is not a good horse,
how can it succeed?

5 .

Case

The World-Honored One takes up his seat. Manjusri in-vites the bell to sound and announces, "Listen to the Dharma of the Dharma King. The Dharma King's Dharma is thus."

Commentary

On a zither without strings, the music of spring is playing. Its notes are heard throughout space and time.

Verse

Each word is impeccable,
but one sees a tail-piece that cannot be hidden.
Here is a flute without holes
playing the universal song of peace.

6 .

Case

Sword in hand, the Emperor of the Tan Kingdom interro-gates the twenty-fourth Ancestral Teacher: "Are you clear

about the emptiness of the five skandhas [aggregates]?" "Yes,"
replies the teacher. "Have you crossed over birth and death?"
"Yes," he replies. "Can you give me your head?" "This body
does not belong to me, how much less this head." The Emperor beheads him. White milk gushes from the severed head.
The Emperor's arm falls.

Commentary

The sword at the neck of the knight beheads the spring
breeze.

Verse

The sharp blade sweeps through the air like lightning.
When we are aware of it, we have nothing to fear.
I will depart this morning.
I leave the country of waters and mist,
but no one can be sure a thought isn't still hidden
beneath.

7 .

Case

Great Master Bodhidharma goes to the Thieu Lam pagoda
at Lac Duong. For nine years he sits facing the wall.[1]

---

[1] Beginning here, we use the Vietnamese transliteration of Chinese names,
in the tradition of the Vietnamese study of these Kung-ans.

Commentary

Watch out, don't just sleep!

Verse

The giant bird has gone thousands of miles
to reach the southern sea
and then regrets the long distance traveled.
Last night we drank too much at the Great Festival.
This morning, it's difficult to wake up.

8 .

Case

The Second Ancestral Teacher begs Bodhidharma to pacify his mind. Bodhidharma says, "Show me your mind, and I
will pacify it for you." The Second Teacher replies, "I have
looked and looked, but I cannot find it!" Bodhidharma answers, "Your mind has been pacified."

Commentary

Crowned with garlands, the three-year-old child plays the
drum. The eighty-year-old man plays with a balloon.

Verse

If mind is not-mind, who can we ask for advice?
Is it possible to become a fetus again?
The old monk who thinks he can calm the mind of
    another

is just mocking everyone around him,
and he doesn't even know it.

9 .

Case

Manjusri notices a woman sitting in a trance near the Buddha. He tries to wake her up, but in vain. The Buddha then
asks Vong Minh to wake her up, and he does it in just one
stroke.

Commentary

This horror has destroyed my whole fortune.

Verse

Facing Buddha, no discrimination is possible.
The trance does not appear to be real.
If nature does not pick or choose,
when spring comes here, it must be spring everywhere.

1 0 .

Case

During the thirty years of the Ho War, Master Ma To Dao
Nhat never lacked for salt or soy sauce.

Commentary

This declaration is impeccable, but the challenge is to eat with your fingers while holding on to your chopsticks.

Verse

Since becoming the friend of a drunkard,
he has taken the liquor store as his home.
When you brag about being a great knight,
you play forever the role of a man without a shirt?

1 1 .

Case

Bach Truong returns to Ma To for another interview. Ma To lets out a yell. Bach Truong is enlightened.

Commentary

Better one blow with a pickax than a thousand taps with a mattock.

Verse

Formerly, when Way and Book
were not yet confused,
I heard on all sides
the humming of bees.
Now, on my horse,
with my sword in hand,

I have perfect oneness
on the Way of Truth.

1 2 .

Case

The National Teacher calls his assistant three times, and three times his assistant replies, "I am here." "I thought," says the master, "I had transgressed against you, but in fact it is you who have transgressed against me."

Commentary

Only the one who drinks knows exactly whether the drink is warm or cold.

Verse

Both parties have the same talent.
On whom can we rely for a comparison?
My lungs and entrails are available for your inspection,
but I alone know my true situation.

1 3 .

Dai Quy says, "The concepts *being* and *nonbeing* are like clinging vines that cannot survive on a great tree." So Son replies, "If the tree is cut down, if the vines are dried out, where will the concepts *being* and *nonbeing* go?" Dai Quy walks out with a great burst of laughter.

Commentary

Water remains in the sea. The moon is in the sky.

Verse

The sea is calm when the wind stops blowing.
Still, we search outside of ourselves.
One burst of laughter dissipates a thousand doubts.
Pearls are distinguished from stones.

1 4 .

Case

Bach Truong asks Nam Tuyen, "What is the Dharma preached for the non-benefit of people?" Nam Tuyen answers, "It is not the mind. It is not the Buddha. It is not anything."

Commentary

Thousands of wise ones have searched, but the Dharma has left not a single trace. They are all hiding in great space.

Verse

The kung-an is there, standing before you.

Face it squarely, look at it!

Do you understand?

When invited to stay in the Buddha's hut,

we always refuse.

We are too used to sleeping among the rushes.

1 5 .

Case

Nam Tuyen says, "Mind is not the Buddha. Wisdom is not the Way."

Commentary

I yearn for the soul of marvelous truth.

Coming back to myself, I walk beneath the shining moon.

Verse

Stars move with silent sounds.

The universe is calm, nothing brings trouble.

Leaning on a staff, I climb up to the terrace.

Perfect tranquillity: nothing whatsoever is happening.

Case

To instruct his disciples, Master Lam Te uses only a stick. Each time he sees a monk, he shouts.

Commentary

At noon on the fifth day of the fifth month, all the poisons of the mouth and tongue are neutralized.

Verse

Having scarcely arrived at the door, one hears the yell.
Children and adolescents wake up.
The first thunder clap in spring.
Everywhere the green buds burst forth on the branches.

1 7 .

Case

Master Nam Tuyen says, "Everyday thought is the Way."

Commentary

If it is cold, say "cold." If it is warm, say "warm."

Verse

The precious stone has an immaculate nature.
Its beauty does not depend on the work of a good
    jeweler.

If the road back is not followed,
you may fall deep into the valley.

1 8 .

Case

Master Trieu Chau says, "You are controlled by the twenty-four hours of the day. I control the twenty-four hours of the day!"

Commentary

He calls himself a master and yet he despises people. His speech has no basis whatsoever.

Verse

The old man kids himself.
He says he can tame fiery dragons and ferocious tigers
twenty-four hours a day.
In fact, if one knows how to change iron into gold,
he won't go telling everyone he meets in the street.

19.

Case

A monk questions Lam Te, "What is *the true person of no rank?*" Lam Te replies, "Dried excrement."

Commentary

Aiming at a sparrow with an unloaded rifle. Hitting a mouse with a stick he doesn't want to stain!

Verse

The true person of no rank is nothing but dried
  excrement.
How practitioners must be led astray by such a
  teaching!
Look and consider again!
Don't you see it yet?
When the clay buffalo walks in the sea, there are no
  footprints.

20.

Case

Master Trieu Chau says, "I have found the old lady of the Ngu Dai Son Mountain."

Commentary

Whoever has committed the five major crimes is forbidden to cover his ears when thunder roars.

Verse

> In the wink of an eye, Ngu Dai Son Mountain has
>   disappeared.
> Without walking for days, one is suddenly at home.
> If the war is ended and no one dreams of vengeance,
> what need is there of taking the sword from its sheath?

2 1 .

Case

Golden buddhas cannot save the crucible, nor wooden buddhas the fire, nor clay buddhas the water. The true Buddha is sitting calmly in the sanctuary.

Commentary

Mountains are mountains, rivers are rivers. Where is the Buddha?

Verse

> If Cuong Xuyen's picture has such renown,
> it is thanks to the poet Vuong Duy.
> I also have talent, but why must I paint?
> Looking into space, see the moon
> and feel the cool freshness of the wind.

Case

Master Trieu Chau says, "When I was at Thanh Chau, I made a linen robe that weighed seven pounds."

Commentary

Thanh Chau's radishes are okay, but Thanh Chau's linen only upsets people!

Verse

What a very spectacular linen robe!
How could Trieu Chau's bamboo trunk contain a robe
    like that?
Even if you meticulously distinguish between ounces
    and half-ounces,
you hold all eight Manh brothers up to scorn.

Case

On being asked if a dog has the Buddha nature, Trieu Chau replies "yes" once, and "no" another time.

Commentary

Two choices, one chance.

Verse

> When confronted by people, you can say yes or no.
> A single word routs Ho's army.
> He who boasts all his life of being brilliant
> is only an obscure relative of the true knight.

2 4 .

Case

Master Trieu Chau says, "Where the Buddha resides, do not stop. Where the Buddha does not, pass quickly by!"

Commentary

When water collects, it makes a pool. When a stick strikes the earth, it leaves its mark.

Verse

> Residing, not residing—the two do not reside at all.
> Words are never perfect.
> After the flower was held up to the assembly, the fact
>   could be recounted.
> But in Buddha's country one arrives without taking even
>   a single step.

Case

Showing his bamboo cane, Master Thu Son says, "Call this a bamboo cane, and you have entered my trap. Do not call it a bamboo cane, and you fall into error. What do you call it?"

Commentary

Don't move! Whoever moves gets thirty blows!

Verse

It is difficult to choose between cane and non-cane.
Who can give a clear reply?
The Way is always there,
but obstacles are always encountered.

Case

A monk asks Dong Son, "What is the Buddha?" Dong Son replies, "Three pounds of linen hanging on the wall."

Commentary

To call (Buddha) a thing is not correct.

Verse

> What is the Buddha?
> The three pounds of linen Dong Son hung on his wall.
> Even if people stop speculating,
> we still have to use things
> to point out the truth.

2 7 .

Case

"What was Great Ancestor Bodhidharma's intention?" a monk asked Hien Tu. Hien Tu answered, "The liquor table before the spirits' shrine."

Commentary

A lion's cub should not run after an avalanche.

Verse

> When its roots are cut, the tree is felled.
> I tell you what I have seen with my own eyes.
> To say, "The Great Ancestor's intention is the liquor
>   table in front of the shrine"
> is to say, "Pants are trousers!"

2 8 .

Case

National Master Vo Nghiep says, "If a discrimination is made between enlightenment and non-enlightenment, even as fine as the tip of a hair, it will cause people to be reborn as horses and donkeys." The monk Bach Van Doan replies, "Even if this discrimination between enlightenment and non-enlightenment disappears, people will still be born horses and donkeys."

Commentary

If you burn the forest, the tigers will flee. If you beat at the bushes, the snakes will be afraid.

Verse

What a dumb statement!
Why bother to beat the bushes to make snakes afraid?
If you know the road to the capital,
you won't have to ask anyone.

2 9 .

Case

Master Huyen Sa says to the Assembly, "The Honored Ones often speak of their efforts intending to show people the

Way of Emancipation. But how would you show a deaf, dumb, and blind man the Way? . . . If you hold up your whisk, he will not see it. If you tell him about sitting meditation, he will not hear you. If you try to get him to recite the sutras, he will not be able to utter a single word."

Commentary

When we are hungry, we eat. When we are thirsty, we drink. When it is cold, we cover ourselves. When it is warm, we fan ourselves.

Verse

When we are sad, we cry, and when we are joyful, we
    laugh.
Nose vertical, eyebrows horizontal.
Hunger, thirst, warmth, and cold, are natural.
Why create problems that don't exist?

3 0 .

Case

Master Thuy Nghiem often said to himself, "Wake up! Wake up! Don't let anyone despise you for another moment."

Commentary

It's too much trouble to cry until blood starts to gush from your mouth. It is much better to shut up and wait until spring has passed.

Verse

> Thuy Nghiem often said to himself, "Wake up!"
> But he was not truly courageous!
> If he was really such a hero,
> why didn't he grab the sun and throw it down onto the
>   earth?

3 1 .

Case

"I will enter the world of politics," says Tam Thanh, "and a great statesman will arise. But I will not enter the world of politics for him." Hung Hoa replies, "If a great statesman should arise, I will not enter the world of politics. But if I were to enter the world of politics, I would do it for him."

Commentary

A blind tortoise encounters two paralyzed brethren.

Verse

> If you are thirsty, don't drink dirty water.
> Food alone will not fill your stomach.
> If a child licks the sugar off the knife
> he may well cut his tongue.

3 2 .

Case

    When Dang An Phong arrives, Master Nam Tuyen shows him a vase and says, "This vase is an object. Don't be attached to it."

Commentary

    If an object exists, what is there to be attached to?

Verse

    The clearness of the mirror
    has nothing to do with dust.
    Why work so hard to get rid of dust?
    Just enjoy each moment.
    When you finish your dinner, have a cup of tea.

3 3 .

Case

    Master Tach Dau says, "It cannot be left thus; it cannot not be left thus; it can neither be left thus nor not be left thus."

Commentary

    Everything is impermanent. Suffering exists.

Verse

I have a touching story to tell you.

But please wait until this cloud passes our grotto.

Otherwise, even if I tell the story perfectly,

the distance between us will still be ten thousand miles.

3 4 .

Case

A monk asks Master Giap Son, "How is it, Giap Son's world?" "Carrying his little one in his arms, the monkey returns to his virgin forest, while the flower petals cover the ground of the green valley."

Commentary

Take a cane with you, and you will tapdance everywhere there are people.

Verse

No one has visited the distant world of Giap Son.

But you must do so.

Those who are enlightened,

who see through the eyes of great wisdom,

can see noon at midnight.

3 5 .

Case

A monk asks Master Muc Chau, "Can the entire Buddhist Canon be read in the time of one breath?" Muc Chau replies, "If Tat La, the cake seller, comes by, tell him to come in."

Commentary

One arrives home without even walking.

Verse

The Canon read in the time of a breath.
No need to consider each word or phrase.
The deepest truths disclose themselves naturally;
don't even ask the hermit on the hill.

3 6 .

Case

One day, in the presence of Master Lam Te, two senior monks started to yell at each other at the same time. A novice asked Lam Te, "In the present case, is there a distinction between the consultor and consulted?" Lam Te replied, "Both are here."

Commentary

White monkeys with bizarre gesticulations.

Verse

The voice of the Enlightened One can be heard in the
wind,
the meaning of a kung-an is not outside.
Lam Te knows how to measure land and rice paddies.
He divides them into lots and distributes them to
everyone.

37.

Case

Master Huyen Sa said, "I am like the owner of a piece of
land, and at the center I have planted a tree. I want to sell the
land, but keep the tree."

Commentary

The Great Ocean is not big enough for a single corpse.

Verse

Even if you are enlightened,
even if thoughts have ceased to assail you,
there still remains one small point to resolve—
Is it correct to consider gold and silver as dust?

Case

A monk asked Master Hue Tu, "What is the essence of Buddhism?" Hue Tu replied, "What is the price of rice at Lu Lang?"

Commentary

The shadow of bamboo sweeps the floor of the veranda, but the dust doesn't move.

The moon is reflected in the water, but there is no trace left on the surface of the pond.

Verse

The speech is worthy of a warrior.
It corresponds well to the mentality of the people
and helps them on the Way of Liberation.
What is the price of rice at Lu Lang?
If you knew it, you would no longer have to cross
the distance of a thousand miles.

3 9 .

Case

A monk asks Van Thu Vien Minh, "All things enter the One. But what does the One enter?" Van Thu replies, "The Hoang Ha River has nine sections."

Commentary

The countryside was so beautiful, I didn't realize my boat had already passed Thuong Chau.

Verse

I tell you of the nine sections of the Hoang Ha River,
to help you return home without having to cross such a
    great distance.
But you have not taken your eyes off the outstretched
    net,
and so don't even notice the birds passing overhead.

4 0 .

Case

Master Nam Tuyen asks Trieu Chau, "Novice, do you have a master?" Trieu Chau answers, "Yes, I already have a master." Nam Tuyen asks, "What does it mean to have a master?" Trieu

Chau rubs his hands and replies politely, "Today it is cold. I hope that the Venerable One enjoys the greatest well-being."

Commentary

For someone with agile hands, needles can replace cudgels.

Verse

> While rubbing his hands, Trieu Chau shows us
> that which stands between the two extremes of
>   consultor and consulted.
> Is it not Hoa Lam's and Han Lenh's subterfuge,
> if Hoi has retired from the contest?

4 1 .

Case

A monk asks Master Moc Am, "It is said that the monk's robe, made of scraps of cloth, is not worth very much. What does that mean?" "A needle," replied Moc Am, "cannot go through it."

Commentary

In the perfect state of meditation, all discriminations are absent. Even a thread cannot find its way in empty space.

Verse

> The monk's robe is soft like snow,
> but needles of steel cannot pierce it.

Space is one, without a crack:
By what road does the scent of the cinnamon flowers
come to us at the end of the day?

4 2 .

Case

The layman Lung declares, "This is Buddha's examination.
Those who pass the test of emptiness will be declared winners."

Commentary

For your name to be on the list of winners, don't leave
blank pages.

Verse

Can one make straw sandals
with the feathers of a bird?
Can one become a Buddha
by taking part in this strange competition?
Stay on guard! Don't go and say
that you will be crowned
after you have passed the test of emptiness.
If you do, sooner or later you will receive
great blows of a stick.

4 3 .

Case

Master Tu Minh asks Chan Diem Tru, "What is the essence of Buddhism?" Chan Diem Tru replies, "Clouds that form at the peak of the mountain do not exist, but the reflection of the moon in the water does." Tu Minh roars, "You have been practicing for so many years and you still answer so stupidly!" Chan Diem Tru began to weep and a moment later, says to Tu Minh, "It is obvious that I do not know what the essence of Buddhism is. I beg you to clarify it for me." Tu Minh declares, "The clouds that are formed at the peak of the mountain do not exist, but the reflection of the moon in the water does." Hearing these words, Chan Diem Tru is transformed, and reaches enlightenment.

Commentary

Compassionate ones think it is humanism. Wise ones think it is erudition.

Verse

The music you play is equally mine.
Good friends know each other thoroughly.
Mountain above, river below,
but moon and clouds remain the same.

ADDITIONAL READING

For a catalog of all books and tapes by Thich Nhat Hanh or a current schedule of his lectures and retreats worldwide, please contact:

Parallax Press
Community of Mindful Living
P.O. Box 7355
Berkeley, CA 94707

DATE DUE
